Acknowledgements

No book, however individually created, ever makes it to print without dragging virtually every friend, acquaintance, and often people who were former friends before you came up with the book idea into the fray. Thanks to all of you.

Special mention to Nate Niles former calculus teacher who at 86 can still spot an errant comma from 100 feet who invested hours editing the manuscript. Patty Allen who put up with my frustrations without complaint. Darla Lynn Pfenninger of Gem Literary Services, tireless literary agent who struggled to get this published through normal channels. Now we're trying unconventional channels to see if they work any better.

Finally, trusted dog Edi who patiently lay at my feet while I struggled to urge words onto a blank computer screen.

Do you give a Cold Shower or a Warm Bubble Bath?

Dave

Best Wishes

Do you give a Cold Shower or a Warm Bubble Bath?

Marketing Secrets They Don't Cover In MBA Programs

By "The Marketing Guy" Leon Frank

Additional copies of this book can be purchased at www.lulu.com/marketingsecrets.

The author may be reached at lfrank@membersnow.com.

Dedication

To Dorothy and Leon Frank
You know why!

Contents

Introduction

If you're good at what you do but frustrated at the complexities of having to sell what you do, this book was written for you. You went into business specifically so you could provide a better service or a better product than what was already on the market. Now you have to sell that better service or product.

Back in the fifties if you had plunked down your savings and opened Herb's Corner Grocery (if your name was Herb that is), your strategy for success would have been pretty straightforward. Smile at the customers and make sure the stuff they wanted was on your shelves. Simply doing those two things would not only ensure success, but would have turned you into a pillar in your community to boot. No one even mentioned the term marketing back then. Your marketing program was smiling at customers and making sure the shelves were stocked. After forty years of smiling and stocking, you could retire with the same feather duster tucked in your back pocket and bunches of money tucked in your savings account.

That business model ended with the Cleavers.

In today's hostile business climate, your competitors get up each morning with the single goal of taking your customers away from you. If you sit back and follow the "smile and keep it on the shelf" rule, you'll soon have trouble paying the rent. Forget being a pillar of the community.

Today, business goes to the company with the solid marketing program far more then to the one with solid products. How you sell what you do is far more important than how you do what you do.

Most business managers find the process of marketing their products and services daunting. There's so much to know and no place to learn it other than in the trenches. Using the trial and error method can be lethal. You can easily go through your entire prospective client universe while you try to get it right.

Selling is a courtship. And like courting, the rules tend to be always in flux. Should you send flowers? Should you send a thank you note? How soon should you call after the last meeting? Guess wrong dating and you blow the courtship. Guess wrong in business and you may not be able to pay the mortgage.

There are so many strategies to learn. What do you do if your proposal comes in second? How do you combat rumors spread by your competitors? How do you capitalize on the success of a star salesperson?

This book offers creative solutions you won't learn in business courses. By using them, you will increase sales effectiveness without increasing your advertising costs. Either you or your competitors is going to stay up nights worrying about falling revenues. Make it your competitors. With the secrets in this book, you'll take their clients away from them, not the other way around.

You work hard to produce your products and services. Here's how to sell them.

Would You Rather Have a Cold Shower or a Warm Bubble Bath?

Picture this.

It's twilight, that magical time of evening when the setting sun sparkles across the field next to your house. You step into a sunken marble bathtub filled with warm water sudsing with lilac bubble bath. You slip down in the tub and let the water rise up to your neck. You sip champagne from a crystal flute. You look out the window and gaze across wildflowers glowing in the fading sunlight. The sinking sun slowly streaks the sky crimson as it inches towards the treetops. Fragrant candles flicker around the edge of the tub. A fountain splashes into the tub adding soothing waterfall sounds to the classical music wafting from hidden stereo speakers. Ice cream bonbons are in a cut glass bowl by your side. You pop one into your mouth. The troubles of the day fall away as you lose yourself in the evening.

As you picture that soothing feeling, compare it to this one:

You jump into a cold shower in a bare stall, wash quickly with lye soap, then hop out onto a cold tile floor and dry off with a scratchy too small towel.

Is there any difference between the two experiences?

Both get the same job done – scrubbing the body clean. Yet there's a huge emotional gulf between a warm bubble bath and a cold shower. Which experience would you enjoy more? Which experience do you think your customers enjoy more?

When customers do business with your company, what is the emotional feeling you provide? Is it a warm bubble bath or a cold shower? When you provide your services and products, are you thoroughly professional, competent, and cold? Clients want you to get the job done. But they'd enjoy doing business with you far more if the experience matches a sunken marble tub rather than a bare shower stall.

In today's competitive market, simply being good is not a competitive advantage, your competitors do the job well too. To outdo the competition, you must make the experience of doing business with you a positive emotional experience. Add emotional warmth to the way you serve your clients and you'll immediately stand out from your competitors.

Give your company the Cold Shower Test. Take a sheet of paper and list each step of client contact. Include everything: initial greeting, sales presentation, proposal, taking the order, delivery of the product, invoicing, post sale follow-up. Each time you and your customer connect, write it down.

Now go back through your list and give each step a numerical rating for warmth and friendliness. If your customer is treated with the equivalent of a nice bubble bath, rate it a 5. If it's equivalent to a cold shower stall, give it a 1.

How did you score? If you didn't make it out of the teens, you have a great deal of work to do. And you'd better hurry before your clients find out it's much more bubble bathy over at your competitors.

Here are a few pointers for making your business feel more like a warm bubble bath than a cold shower:

Add Stuff – think of that marble tub full of sudsy water I described at the beginning. Everything listed was added specifically for the feeling. The bubble bath, the candles, champagne, bonbons. Even the sunken tub next to the windows was built just to make the experience enjoyable. Build niceties into your customer's experience. Add things that have nothing to do with getting the job done, but are there only to enhance the customers pleasure.

Bare is bad – unlike the bath where body bareness is prerequisite, bare is bad in business. What does your paperwork look like? Are they plain legal documents? Are your proposals filled with numbers? Bad, bad, bad. These are all cold showers by themselves. Add some warmth. The 7-page contract is just as legal when presented in a colorful folder with photographs. Put some life into it.

Food is Good – we all love to eat. A simple bowl of hard candy on your counter can actually increase business. Use food also to slow down customers so you can sell them more. People are less eager to leave when they are eating. Serve lunch. Give drinks. Make popcorn. Offer donuts. Their waistline is their problem. Your problem is making them very happy they visited.

Flowers work too – whether your customers are men or women, a flower is a positive surprise. Women keep it; guys give it to the woman in their life. Everyone benefits. Consider the corner mechanic who leaves a long stem rose on the seat of every client's car. His clients tell everyone at work the next day around the water cooler. He receives far more publicity than if he spent the cost of the flowers for advertising.

Make your proposals alive – When you write your proposal, you are most concerned about the numbers. This is how much you'll get paid for doing the work. Your clients look at it in the other direction. To them, your proposal is a description of the benefits they will receive from paying you. They want to anticipate those benefits by having them spelled out in your proposal. Create proposals that lift the client's expectations. Elaborate on the benefits they will receive by signing the order.

Be Creative – Let your creative juices run wild. If you're selling your prospects on a trip to Mexico, serve your proposal in a fringed straw Sombrero with chips and salsa. Guess which proposal clients will remember when your competitors sent theirs in a plain envelope?

Enthusiasm – Call your own phone number. Does the voice that answers sound like they've been embalmed? If so, you're presenting prospects with a cold shower before they even meet you. Train your receptionist to answer each call like it's the most exciting event of the day. Work on your own answering machine message. If you aren't enthusiastic when you had time to rehearse before hand, what are you like in real life?

Everyone's life is already filled with too many cold showers already. Scheduling the dishwasher repair and sitting there waiting for , "sometime between 8AM and noon." Juggling a staff meeting with the kid's soccer game. Waiting thirty minutes on hold for tech support. Snippy cashiers at the grocery store. No one wants more cold water in their life.

Make your company different. Stand out from cold and professional by being warm and professional. Offer a warm bubble bath. People will do business with you just for the sheer enjoyment of it.

Warm bubble bath or cold shower? Both get the job done. But you'll have a lot more customers if you serve warm bubbles along with your products.

Try Selling as a Consultant

George McNeil is tall, handsome, and articulate. He carries 20 years experience of corporate management under his belt. He has the credentials to handle himself easily in the business world.

He recently switched careers. He began representing a product he had used in his corporate life. Armed with a war chest of true-life anecdotes, he headed out to conquer the sales arena. He should make the ideal sales person for this product. He makes a convincing case for the product's value. Yet his success has been less than spectacular. He can't sell worth a damn. He is now revisiting the decision to change careers.

For George, several factors combined to bury his sales career. The first was an expectable lack of selling skills coming from his previous life on the other side of the desk. He had always been the buyer. Although he had seen the good, the bad and the ugly of sales presentations, translating those observations into his own selling style was not easy.

So he signed up for a sales training course. This right sounding decision turned out to be his second problem. He landed in the used car section of selling school.   The techniques they taught were fine for a pawnshop -- they didn't work at all with CEO's.

Matching selling techniques to your audience is vital to your end results.   As George quickly learned, attempting to close using the procedures that work for aluminum siding when offering a $10,000 professional service does not yield sales.   It results in far more offended prospects than signed purchase orders.

George   now   is   switching   sales   strategies   to Consultative   Selling.   This   much   more   appropriate methodology treats the prospect with respect and is far more successful in the high level corporate environment. Here's how it works:

Think of yourself as a consultant, not a salesman. This is a major mindset change.   You are a hired gun brought in to solve a problem.   Your first (and only) consulting assignment is to determine if your products or services are right for the prospect you are calling on.   Go in to the sales presentation, not hoping they choose you, but as an objective professional who was called in to examine their needs.   You are the Doctor conducting a check up.   You will provide them with your consulting expertise on one decision: whether your products or services are right for them.   In this field you are the top expert.   You know more about this subject than anyone else in the meeting.

Conduct your sales presentation as a fact gathering meeting.   Start by accumulating information.   Ask about their needs. Ask specific questions about current vendors. The first thing a good consultant does is become familiar with the company they are trying to help.   Learn their company.   Learn their strengths and weaknesses.   Learn the problems they deal with and how your services or products can solve those issues.   Prepare a list of specific questions to ask any potential client.   The answers to these questions will provide you with information you need to make an informed recommendation.

Among the questions you want answered is other alternatives they are considering.   These are called competitors in your lexicon. One of your consulting tasks is to determine if a competitor offers better value than your company does (if so, you are working for the wrong company). Keep in mind alternatives they are considering include doing it in house and doing nothing. Learn what options are on the table.

Once you understand their operation, their needs, and the competing options they are considering, make your recommendation. Will they truly be served by purchasing your services? You are the authority. Here is where you earn your consulting merit badge.

Is your stuff right for them? If so, how will it benefit them? What advantages will they derive from purchasing from you rather than any of the other options under consideration (including doing nothing)? What about timing. Is this the right time to bring you on board or do certain events need to be accomplished first? Based on what you learned about their needs and operation, you should now have a clear picture of whether your products will help them.

If your products or services are NOT right for them, say so. Explain why and recommend what you think is their best alternative. Don't worry about losing the sale.   They'll be so impressed with your professionalism; they'll send a ton of referrals your way.

Assuming your products or services are right for them, announce your decision. Here you are the specialist rendering an expert opinion. Provide your conclusions clearly and resolutely. This is a decision point in the meeting. You have solved their problems.

Now, keeping in the consultant role, demonstrate why this is the correct business decision for them. Present a written comprehensive report (your proposal). Explain in detail how your products and services will benefit their operation. Cover every point that's been discussed in an objective, consultative format. Remember, you are not trying to convince them to buy – you are showing them the benefits of making the purchase decision.

Look at each prospect from the mindset of a consulting assignment. Objectively evaluate whether your products are right for them and if they are, demonstrate why. As a consultant, your role is education. You're the expert remember? If your products are the right business decision for them at this time and they don't buy from you, you've failed to do your job of educating them. Once you evaluate their operation and come to a professional conclusion that their business would be more successful using your products and services, it's your task to teach them why.

Congratulations – you've just been promoted. You are no longer a salesman. You've been elevated to providing expert advice and counsel as a consultant. Your pay raise will come with the additional signed orders you bring in.

Cold Call Therapy

You say you don't like making Cold Calls. The thought of picking up the phone and dialing a complete stranger makes you break out in a sweat. Come, lie down on the sofa, relax, and tell me all about it. Dr. Marketing Guy will help you.

Let's talk about why you'd rather get a heart transplant than make a Cold Call:

- You think all people who make Cold Calls should be given a final cigarette and then be shot at sunrise by a 5 man firing squad.

- You resent eating cold mashed potatoes as a result of having your supper interrupted by peddlers trying to sell you everything from cemetery plots to replacement windows.

- You can't imagine inflicting yourself on other unsuspecting victims.

- You consider it unprofessional and demeaning. After all pediatricians don't build their practices by calling recent mothers prospecting for new patients.

Now let Dr. Marketing Guy help you overcome this Cold Call phobia. We'll start by looking at it from the other end of the telescope.

Imagine sitting at your desk agonizing over the announcement you're about to make canceling the employee health insurance program. The phone rings. You pick it up and hear, "Sir, I have great news for you! We're offering group health insurance at very competitive rates. Would you like me to give you a proposal?"

As a result, you save enough to maintain the company insurance program.

Was it a Cold Call that just saved your health insurance? Because it brought you something good, you don't consider it a negative. Yet, it was truly a Cold Call. What you have to realize is, not all Cold Calls are a blight on the landscape. Many Cold Calls are happily received. It depends on the call, the caller, and the message.

So let's consider the cemetery plot salesman who routinely ruins your mashed potatoes and look at what he does wrong to help us do it right. Here are some Cold Calling tips that will create a calling environment where both parties enjoy the experience.

How are you today? -- If you don't know the person you're calling, never, never, never ask, "How are you?" It signals a Cold Call and strikes a defensive relationship right at the start. Besides, they and you both know you couldn't care less how they are.

A little respect please – The strongest objection to an intrusive Cold Call is the lack of respect. The caller takes hold of the conversation and won't let go just in case you're trying to say your kid just fell down 3 flights of stairs and you were sort of hoping to keep the phone line free until the ambulance arrived. When you make your own Cold Calls, ask if this is a good time to talk. If it's not, ask when you can call back.

Use a script – Professionals who have trained, studied, and have successfully been making Cold Calls for years use a script. You need one too. Write it out and rehearse it before you hit the phones. Record yourself doing the call and listen attentively. Work on phrasing, inflection, and tone of voice. All convey clearly to the listener.

Come right to the point – Don't waste their time or more important, yours. Use direct questions to find out immediately if they are a prospect. Do they have any need for your products or services? If not, get off the phone so both of you can get on with your lives.

Bring something good – A bad Cold Call is one the recipient didn't want. Bring something good with your call. Bring new information. Tell ways to save money. Use a real life example. Read excerpts from a newspaper article. Explain why doing business with your company is a good thing. "Newsweek just published a survey that nearly all businesses pay 48% more than they need to on shipping. How do you ship your products?"

What now – What are you trying to sell in the call? Know exactly what action you want them to take before you pick up the phone. Do you want an appointment? Say so. "Ms. Melloch, our new procedure is perfect for Acme Bowling Balls. When may I come by and show you our drilling machines?"

Relax and enjoy it – Every person you call is human. They weren't sure what tie or blouse to wear today. They worried the staff meeting would extend past pickup time at the day care center. Their car needs an oil change. They deal with too much boring stuff through the day already. Don't let your call be boring on top of their daily routine! Bring a song into their life. Be funny, witty and enjoyable. Whether someone is a prospect for your company or not, make sure they enjoy the few minutes they spend talking to you.

Cold Calls don't have to be terrible. They can be enjoyable and rewarding to both the caller and the recipient. It depends on the preparation you put into it and what you offer. Work to make your calls enjoyable and professional. They will be successful for you and the people you call.

By the way, do you need a set of encyclopedias? This guy keeps calling me every night.............

What's wrong with General Motors

Last year, my dad bought a 3 year old Buick Park Avenue which he had watched his widow neighbor baby for its entire life. When she traded in the car, he was standing on the lot waiting. The car had every bell and whistle and best of all, only 22,000 miles on the engine. Dad looked forward to many years of enjoying the car.

The many years came up short, however, when the transmission ground itself to pieces six thousand miles later. No problem, my dad thought. He was still far short of the 36,000 mile warranty. Not so fast, said the dealer. While the car was well short of the mileage warranty, it had exceeded a time warranty of 36 months. No dice on helping with the $2500 repair bill.

Dad's retired so he had hours to devote to arguing with faceless GM wonks trying to find one who believed as he did that the transmission should not turn into mush at the 28,000 mile mark on a $40,000 car. Each one concentrated on the fine print in the warranty rather than the relationship with the customer. Dad finally found one who relented and offered to pay half - $1250. Dad ponied up the other half and drove away with a new transmission singing in the car if not necessarily a new song humming in his heart.

A month later, a routine General Motors survey called to see if he was happy with the repair. Still seething over having to pay for it in the first place, dad jumped on a new audience for his grievance and blasted the poor survey lady. She took it in stride and promised to have someone look into it. A few months later, GM unbelievably coughed up the other $1250 for the repair work.

In my entire business career, I've never heard a more extraordinary example of disastrous customer service. General Motors made a lasting critic out of my dad who tells the story to everyone he knows. Inevitably Dad's travails must have turned people away from GM products. Then in an incredible lose/lose scenario, GM paid the full bill anyway. They ruined a customer relationship, spread the word that they made unreliable products, then paid in full. If they had fixed the transmission immediately with no hassle, they'd have spent the same amount of money with a customer singing their praises. The net result would have been several new customers. People can live with the mechanical issues. It's the not standing behind it that aggravates.

Dad's previous loyalty to the GM auto family was his loyalty to our own family. My brother works for GM. As part of his employment, he, a mid level manager, receives a new car every 6000 miles. He pays not one cent for it, including fuel. He is also required to lease a GM auto and replace it every two years. He does this with a phone call to a local dealership who gives him special GM pricing and brings the car to his office. My brother and his wife are always driving a car less than 2 year old and they never set foot in a dealership.

This is the reason why GM is so bone headed in their customer service. No one from the mid level manager up has a clue what owning a GM automobile looks like, feels like or costs like. No one on the executive floor has ever wasted hours pleading with a car manufacturer to fairly honor their warranty.

If GM is serious about fixing their problems, here is what they should do:

Stop the Free Autos: no one, from the CEO to the janitor should receive an auto free or even at a discount from GM. Stop living in a fantasy land and join the real world. You cannot sell to a market place if you don't understand it.

Be Your Own Customer: require everyone from mid level manager up to purchase a new GM product every two years. Let them go through the hassles of bargaining with the dealer, understanding MSRP, and arguing trade in values. Once they've succeeded in buying the car, they can look forward to warranty arguments like the rest of the public.

Live Close to the Edge: The real understanding of car ownership comes from driving naked after the warranties have expired. You're on your own for every repair regardless of whether it resulted from poor workmanship by the car maker. GM should require every manager to purchase a 4 year old GM product from a used car dealer and drive it for 3 more years. Only here, Grasshopper, where the overwhelming majority of your clients live, can you understand the visceral fear of owning the products you manufacture.

Will these changes solve the legacy issues of health care? No, of course not. But GM's legacy problems are exacerbated by their primary problem, dismal car sales. It's driving all the other problems. They continue to design inadequate cars, expect the marketplace to accept them, and then argue with their customers when products fail to measure up to even minimal standards. GM isn't the only company that operates this way, but it's the most public.

If your company insulates your employees from the visceral experience of owning your products, you will soon be dealing with the same issues as GM – declining sales and an inability to respond to market forces. You can do market surveys, but it will be far more productive if the attorney writing your warranty coverage just spent 2 hours futilely trying to get a transmission repaired at 28,000 miles. It feels different when it's your own money, something GM managers have never experienced.

If your managers have a head in the sand understanding of the experience your customers suffer when using your products, change now before it's too late. You'll be amazed at how quickly your products will match your market if your managers are customers too.

Selling to a Group

The sales presentation was textbook wonderful. Rapport bounced off the walls. You prepared the PowerPoint to make it colorful, informative and interesting. The effort paid off handsomely, people were glued to every screen. Enthusiasm oozed out their pores. They asked the right questions, you gave the right answers. Their company would clearly be better off buying from you. By the midpoint the air sang with the understanding that the two of you are going to have a long and happy relationship. You mentally calculated the commission as you drove away.

But when you contacted them the following week, iciness had replaced camaraderie. You had trouble getting them on the phone and when you did, they gave vague answers about when they would be ready to sign up. A month later they stopped taking your calls. You don't know if they signed with a competitor or did nothing. They may have been in love with you during the sales presentation, but the marriage never happened.

This happens too often in selling. Feel good sales presentation leads to No Sale. Did you mistake enjoyment of the presentation as a commitment to purchase? What happened after you left that defeated your sale? Were some of the members of the prospect group against you all along and just didn't show it during the presentation? Did a competitor follow you with a sales presentation they liked better?

The answers to these questions are often only known by the prospect, especially when things turn frosty for follow-up phone calls. All you know is that being entertaining and interesting wasn't enough. You put on a good show, but you didn't close.

Selling to a group is a dicey proposition on a good day. You're trying to explain your products, identify their needs, match needs to products, answer questions, and respond to group dynamics all at once. Typically the room is filled with people you've only just met and you need to answer each individual's concerns about your products before you leave. This is not an easy challenge. Here are some ways to increase your success:

Setting up the meeting – 98% of your "After Presentation" success will come from your before presentation preparation. The more of the answers to these questions you have before walking through their door, the higher your success rate will be:

1. Who will be at the meeting? What is each person's role in the company?

2. Who is the decision-maker? Will they be at the meeting?

3. What is the decision process?

4. How many competing presentations are they listening to?

5. What is their time frame for making a selection?

6. What specific questions do they want answered in the presentation?

7. Are they currently using a similar product or service to yours? If so, what do they like and dislike about it?

8. What is their budget?

Prospects who are seriously considering purchasing will give the answers to these questions beforehand. If the primary decision makers are not in the meeting, you want to encourage them to attend. The best way for them to receive the information is to hear it directly from you, not from their staff trying to remember what you said. However, this is not always possible. Many decision makers use their staff to listen to presentations and bring them the information. If you can't get the decision maker to the meeting, hold it anyway.

Getting to Know You – even though you are smiling at a sea of faces, each person is there as an individual. Treat each person as a separate identity. Call each person by name. One trick is to arrange their business cards in front of you to match where they are sitting. Then you can remember at a glance their name and title when looking at them. To start, ask each person to introduce themselves and to tell you what questions they want answered in today's presentation.

Presenting – during your presentation, it is vital to address every objection, question, and comment that the prospect made. Be sure to demonstrate that your product is THE answer to their needs. Tie your comments to individual questions throughout. For example, "Tom, this is how we solve the issue of quality control you brought up when we discussed your current vendor." "Mary, you wanted faster delivery. Our turnaround time is under 7 days, guaranteed."

When you leave, if prospects are unsure about whether to select you as their vendor, you haven't done your job of educating them on the reasons to choose you.

Closing– it's virtually impossible for a group to make a commitment to purchase in your presence. They want to discuss it among themselves after you leave. And if they've scheduled other vendor presentations, they will inevitably wait until all presentations are made to make a selection. You likely cannot close the sale on this call and come away with a signed order. But don't let that discourage you from asking closing questions. "Trial Close" each person. After the formal presentation, go around the room and "close" each person. "Jim, does our product meet your needs?" "Sue, have I answered all your questions?" "Steve, is this what you had in mind?"

These questions are reasonably non threatening and should inspire more group dynamics. They should also ferret out any deep-rooted objections and identify anyone who is going to vote against you at their decision meeting after you leave. This is the person you need to work on. Get them to voice all of their objections while you are present and can respond to them. If objections come up after you leave, you're a dead duck.

Additional Questions – the secret to great selling is great questions. Here are 7 questions to incorporate into your sales presentation:

- Did any of my competitors show you something that I didn't?

- How do [our products] compare to what you've seen so far?

- Will [our products] meet your needs?

- Are there any additional services you might need we didn't discuss here today?

- How does our price compare with your budget?

- How does our price compare with our competitors' offers?

- What additional information can I provide you to help you to decide to go with us?

These questions give you the opportunity to respond to their objections. Not bringing an objection out into the open does not mean it doesn't exist, it just means you can't respond to it. The competitor may have offered a price 30% better than yours for 50% less deliverables. Find out now what their objections are and put them away.

Selling to a group can be very difficult. It also can be very rewarding. Done well, it results in a whole gang of people singing your praises and the signed order in your hand at the end of the process.

No Grouches Allowed

It snowed over Thanksgiving. We loaded the skis and aimed at Vermont. Time to learn how much our muscles had atrophied from doing little more than stare at a computer screen all year. Picturing ourselves yodeling down alpine slopes, we cruised into the picturesque town of Rutland nestled at the base of Killington's vast mountain. Only one detail stood in our path to the aforementioned yodeling -- we couldn't find the hotel.

Fortunately technology has limited some of the male bashing that normally accompanies these family crises. While I might still refuse to stop and ask directions, I am quite willing to pick up a cell phone.

"Comfort Inn, Rutland's Friendliest Hotel" gushed from the handset. Nice change from "How may I direct your call." I liked them instantly. Directions given, U-turn taken, mileage counted, Comfort Inn sign soon filled the windshield. As we grunted suitcases, jackets, and boot bags into the lobby, we heard, "This must be the Frank party," smiling from the check-in desk. I hadn't actually been conducting a poll, but they had already won the Friendliest Hotel award in my book.

By actual count, there are a kazillion hotels, motels, inns, bed and breakfasts, and condos offering to put you up so you can ski at Killington. The brochure of hotel offerings unfolds nearly to South Dakota. All hotels attempt to distinguish themselves from the competition by offering something more. More hot tubs, better rooms, superior restaurants. Yet this enterprising hotel found a very unique way to stand out from the bedlam – with the self-ascribed title of Rutland's Friendliest. They answered the phone with it, assailed you with it as you checked in, boldly printed it on their letterhead, invoices, and brochures. It was more than just their marketing slogan. It was a way of life with them.

Every staff member, from the maintenance guy who came in to fix the drain in the hot tub to the front desk person who had to round up more towels for us to pop into the hot tub in the first place was, well, very friendly. Each one acted as if they were just thrilled we were staying with them. You tended to linger in the lobby just to hear them greet newcomers with their mantra, "Welcome to Rutland's Friendliest Hotel." What a difference from typical languid hotel staff behavior.

How "Friendly" is your business? Do you have an organized program to surround your customers with friendliness? If not, why not? It certainly isn't the cost. The total cost of the Rutland Comfort Inn's marketing program? I added it up. After extensive calculations and entries into the calculator I came up with a final number.

Exactly Zero. Not one additional dime is spent to be Rutland's Friendliest. Yet, because of their friendly program, we wouldn't think of staying at another hotel at Killington. Are your customers that loyal? Or do they come to you because you're convenient?

Being friendly seems easy enough. It should be taken for granted. Yet if you have any doubts about the difference that results from making friendliness an overt policy, wander north to the Rutland Comfort Inn (skiing at Killington is optional). Then wander into any other hotel in the country. Feel the difference between a cheery

"This must be the Frank party!" and the standard hotel chain greeting of "Next." The positive feeling of warmth draws you in and makes you feel comfortable. As a potential customer you want to do business with them.

There is a wonderful side benefit to the friendliness program – it creates a rivalry of escalating politeness. Being constantly reminded that you are in the Friendliest Hotel stretches you, the customer. You want to rise to the challenge. Who wants to be outdone at being friendly? So, the contest is on. Guests are friendly, the staff outfriendlies them, guests escalate to another level, and so on. Everyone is happier. That inevitably cuts down on employee turnover. Shazam! The friendliness marketing program saves recruiting costs in addition to increasing revenues. Seems well worth the zero cost investment to me.

So how friendly is your business? Could you immediately ascribe yourself the title of your city's friendliest? Or do you have some work to do first? Here are a few ways to earn the title and reap the rewards:

Signage – What feelings does entering your business engender? Is it warm and welcoming or are your signs all prohibitions? *Welcome to Al's* does a whole lot more for the soul than *No Pets*.

Telephones – Do you answer the phone as if your dog just died? Put some life into it. Gush a little. Make every caller feel like you were hoping they would ring in. You may have answered the phone 4000 times already today, but it's the first time that customer has dialed your number – make them glad they did.

Paperwork – Are there cheery messages on your printed pieces or are they just informational? There's no rule that says an invoice has to be all numbers. Add some fun. When something goes to the customer, make it alive with friendliness. You're getting it printed anyway. The extra ink to say Have a Nice Day! is free. Use it!

Attitude – Start a friendliness contest with your customers. See who wins. My bet is you both do.

Taking friendliness to extraordinary levels will quickly distinguish you from your competition and make your entire staff happier to boot. You significantly increase your marketing edge without increasing the cost. Try it, I think you'll find the program very user friendly.

Well we're off skiing again. You know where we'll be staying. We're all looking forward to the adventure. I'm especially excited because there's no chance I'll have to stop and ask for directions. I already know how to find the hotel.

Dear Marine Store

Dear Mr. CEO:

It was one of those glorious spring days. We piled burgers and cole slaw and half the people in the marina on two boats and cruised out to our favorite anchoring spot. I was the lead boat, Arnie drove his brand new Carver behind me.

I started calling Arnie's boat, *The Rochelle*, when we cleared the marina. No answer. The entire 4 miles of the Magothy River was spent with me yammering into my microphone -- to no avail. Rafting up without radio coordination left us with the time tested Nordic tradition of hollering to each other. It was messy, but eventually lines were connected, bumpers were bumping, and guests were migrating between the boats.

I yelled over to Arnie, "How much skill does it take to use a VHF radio?" Although new to boating, Arnie should have at least mastered radio communication by now.

"It's you who didn't answer us. We called you the entire trip," came the immediate reply. Accusations went back and forth like an Abbot and Costello routine for a while until Arnie grabbed a handheld VHF radio and in a terrible German accent yelled, "Now ve learn who transmits and who does not."

Of course after making that much noise of it, it was inevitable that it was my radio that had given up its electronic ghost over the winter. Arnie's radio worked just fine.

The next day, I chomped into your marine store checkbook in hand. I was going to have a working radio before our next outing. Radio purchased, old radio removed, boat bridge torn apart, I started installing my new radio. Bracket screwed down, boat wires ready to connect, I would be back on the air in minutes. Mr. CEO, you'll never guess what happened next. Or rather what didn't happen. In order to save approximately 20 cents in manufacturing costs, you only wired half of the connector plug. The 2 additional pins were supposedly in one of the many parts envelopes rattling around inside the carton, but they were missing in action.

Tech support offered to mail the missing pins. I wanted the radio to work now, not next week. Drove back to your store. I had bought the only unit in stock. No help. In desperation, I popped in to Radio Shack who sold me 4 connector pins for 99 cents. Another hour to insert new pins. Finally, the connector plug was wired and the installation was completed. After an extra 3 hours thanks to your missing pins, the new radio worked fine.

During all that driving, calling, waiting on hold, and rewiring, I thought about ways this could have been prevented. Here are a few ideas I'd like to share with you:

Know thy Customer – Virtually everything you sell has to be installed by your customer, typically a person who has no other mechanical events in his life besides screwing stuff onto his boat. Do you know the sophistication level of your customers? Do you know what tools they have available? Survey your customers to establish their level of installation competency and tool inventory. Then require your suppliers to manufacture products to match your customer profile. My guess is you're selling parts that are way over the competency heads of your clients.

Put Tab A in Slot B – Your instruction manual appears to have been written in 38 seconds. Its total guidance to wiring the plug connector is, "Pins supplied." Your instruction manual is the key to whether someone is going to enjoy this product or not. Do it up proper! Have some fun with it. Build a relationship with your customers at the same time. Use fun drawings. Include cartoons. Make the instruction book an event by itself – one that is enjoyable to read and easy to use.

Chain Saw Please – What tools are needed to complete this installation? Are those tools likely to be part of the normal boat toolbox? Design your products so they use simple tools for installation. Put a list of the tools needed on the outside of the package so the purchaser can determine while he's in your store if he needs to buy additional tools. If your installation calls for something exotic, like a 15/37 Allen wrench, include one in the package.

Do it Yourself – Have one of your staffers install each one of your products. Time them. Did the unit get installed properly? Could they follow the instructions? Did they have the tools they needed in an average toolbox? If they have trouble, guess what it will be like for your customers?

One bag, two bags, three bags full – Your retail store did not have a demo unit available. That meant that customers opened units waiting to be sold to examine the product. Each carton has several cellophane bags of parts rattling around loose. Inevitably some of the bags get misplaced when the unit is repacked. Put all the parts bags into one bag and fasten it so they stay until needed.

Do it right – While you want to be cost competitive, saving pennies in manufacturing costs for a $160 radio seems a bit much. It cost me, the end user several hours in additional effort. I'd have gladly paid a bit more for a unit that gave me no hassle installation.

There are many boat equipment retailers competing for the same boat owner customers. All of you offer much the same products at much the same prices. You could really distinguish your marine store by going one step more. Being known as the company whose products are easiest to install would quickly bring you great recognition. You have a great operation. But some muddled thinking on the product design end is diluting the good you're trying to accomplish serving your customers. Improve product design and instruction manuals, and you'll own the marine business.

Then the next time Arnie and I argue over whose boat equipment is defective, at least I can get the new item installed before he knows it was mine.

Sincerely,
Leon Frank
The Marketing Guy

Family Affair

Eddie started his business 40 years ago and watched it grow to over 200 employees. The business has made him a ton of money. His daughters both grew up with the business and when they finished college, they joined the company. They started at the bottom, as Vice Presidents. It was, after all, their legacy. Recently, Eddie has watched sales and profits fall off dramatically. He hired a consultant to help him bring them back up to snuff. The consultant spent a few weeks looking around then said, "You don't have a business problem. You have a daughter problem!"

Susan started her business in her basement by designing a greeting card line that became so popular it was carried in 20 local stores. That was 15 years ago. Now she has two plants and 65 paychecks to feed every month. Her husband joined her in the business. Later their daughter jumped aboard. When the daughter married, the new husband joined the business as well. Lately things have gotten a bit tight in the checkbook so Susan hired a financial expert to suggest ways to ease cash flow bumps. The expert reported that the glitch in her system was not her Accounts Receivable but her son in law.

Dave worked all his life in real estate. His father was a big time developer and it was natural for Dave to follow him into the business. A few years ago, Dave sensed that the company was not keeping up with trends and suggested branching off to provide several additional services he saw the market demanding. His father agreed and set him up with a new company to do it. Dave was president. He hired 30 staffers and worked night and day to get it up and running. His dad provided constant guidance and a few long weekends as well. The new company has been successful from the strong combination of family experience and dedication of the two principals.

Families. They can bring the best of times and the worst of times. There are many examples of family members putting out 200% and working night and day when the chips were down who saved a business that would have failed if it had to rely on outside employees demanding weekly paychecks and overtime. In other cases, family members taking for granted their birthright privilege of ownership, soak up needed assets and sink the ship.

Is your family involved in your business? If so, is their participation a strength or a weakness? Remember, regardless of what you think, your customers will make their own uncannily accurate determination. Be objective and evaluate your situation right now – don't wait for the marketplace to do it for you. Here are a few questions to ask yourself about each family member who is part of your business:

Would you have hired them if they weren't related to you? This is a biggie! Are your family members expected to meet the same requirements as the rest of your employees? If they aren't reaching the same bar as the rest of the staff, be assured your workforce knows it. Your clients know it too. You have compromised your operation by lowering your standards. How many compromises can you afford?

Did they earn their position through their own merits? Is your family member the best person for the position he or she holds? If not, why not? Is it more important to give your nephew a fancy title on his business card than provide your customers the best service possible? You owe it to yourself, to your company, and to your clients to put the best person possible in each position. Your family members should hold their position because they have higher levels of dedication, skill, and experience than other contenders for the job do. Not because of what's written on their birth certificate.

Are they fireable? Are family employees expected to deliver? Or do they think they are immune from consequence if they don't perform? The safer they feel will lessen their keenness to get the job done. Everyone in your operation should have the same expectation of performance.

Do they understand the entire operation? You worked your way through every position to create your business. Do your family members understand the value of sweeping the floor or answering customer complaints? Assign them to each department for a month or so until they have a complete perspective of what makes the business tick.

Do they have outside experience? One of the worst things you can do is to hire your kids right out of college. Give them the benefit of seeing how another business operates first. Your business is all they've heard about at supper for the past 20 years. Now they are living it themselves. This kind of inbreeding virtually guarantees no new ideas in your operation. Let them go out and experience the world, then bring back what they've learned to help your business grow.

Are they compensated according to the market? Here's another ship sinker. Eddie paid his daughters stratospheric salaries. The daughters immediately developed lifestyles based on their exorbitant income. When things got tight, they couldn't live on a lesser more reasonable salary. Pay family members less than market value throughout the year. Then distribute their share of the profits at the end of the year. If the company has done well, let them earn big time. But don't set the expectation that they will get the fat paychecks even when the money isn't in the till.

Family members can be an enormous asset to your business. They bring dedication, loyalty, and commitment far above that of an outsider. On the other hand, they can be a boulder in the road to success. Then you have to work around them as well as the other business challenges you face. Whether your family members are a plus or a minus will depend a great deal on the terms of their employment and the expectations you set for them at the outset. As family they should deliver more, care more, and be more loyal than any other employee. Treat them not as family members inside the business, but as Super Employees. The more you expect from them, the more success you will both find working together.

The enjoyment of sharing your business success with your children is right at the top of the happiness scale. Do it right and you'll both enjoy the experience.

The Case of the Missing Luggage

They were friends of friends. We would likely never see them again. Coffee and cake were served in the living room. Conversation rambled from topic to topic. One easy question in many, "How was your cruise?"

The answer set us back in our chairs.

"It was terrible! We'll never do business with that cruise line again. We tell everyone we meet how lousy they are so no one else will go on a cruise with them either."

All rambling conversation topics were now firmly planted on one issue. They couldn't wait to tell their story to a new audience. They had ponied up an outrageous sum for a first class cabin on a cruise ship. The price per person staggered my senses. I didn't even know people spent that much for a short vacation. Their combined fare would have bought a car.

On the magic day, they excitedly checked in to their lavish, spacious cabin and were told their luggage would arrive shortly. The ship pulled out, no luggage. The luggage never arrived. They weathered a 10-day cruise in the same polo shirts and jeans they wore on board.

No hurricane could have wreaked the wrath of a woman deprived of her toiletries and clothing for 10 days. On formal night, her husband wore one of those T-shirts with tux painted on it – she stayed in the cabin. As we munched on cakes in their living room, they raved out lurid details of their frustration in trying to cope with the cruise with no clothes. Some 2 months after the event, their anger was still at storm strength.

The cruise ship's Customer Service Department was the final blow. As grievous as the blunder of losing their luggage was, they still could have been saved as customers had the situation been handled properly when they returned home. The Customer Service Department started with an unhappy customer and dealt with them so roughly they were converted into furious former customers at the end of being 'helped.' The Customer Service Department offered a detailed explanation of what happened thinking if they offered a good excuse, the couple would convert back into happy sailors. The luggage was mislabeled on the departing dock, then chased them to each port, always arriving a few hours after the ship had departed. It was, according to Customer Service, an understandable, but regrettable occurrence. Excuses and explanations were not even close to what the customer wanted.

Admittedly, this was a Customer Service challenge from Hell. It was after the fact – nothing could now be done to save the disastrous cruise. There is seemingly no right answer. The customer was very angry and was telling everyone they could find, including complete strangers, about their terrible experience. Plus, from the customer's frame of reference, the problem was inexcusable.

How would you have handled a similar Customer Service problem in your business?

Most companies have a Customer Service department. It may be the owner of the company who handles customer complaints; it may be a full department of trained Customer Service Representatives. Whatever the size of your company and your Customer Service Department, you need some system for dealing with unhappy customers.

The goal of the Customer Service Department is very simple: Convert an unhappy customer who is about to mutiny into a happy one who brings repeat business. Achieving that goal is anything but simple. As in the case of the missing luggage, there are frequently no means at hand to change an unhappy experience into a happy one. How do you convert the angry client into someone who is willing to give you another chance?

Here are some ways to improve your Customer Service Program and make it more effective:

Apology – get the chip off your shoulder and tell them you're sorry. A customer who feels wronged wants to know you regret their situation and that what they suffered is not company policy. It will not hurt your company one whit to say, "We're very sorry this happened to you."

Formalized Procedures – develop written instructions for handling each customer service problem. Too often the Customer Service Department looks to the customer for a solution that will make them happy. The customer has no idea what will make them happy. As in this case, all they can see is the ruined cruise that they had so looked forward to. Develop a formula of compensation for every predictable situation so you aren't reinventing the wheel with each new event.

Investigation – In most cases, you need to do research from your end to find out what did happen. Tell the customer exactly what you are going to do and how long it will be before you get back to them. Then make sure you live up to whatever promises you made.

Communication – keep the customer informed. If it does take a few weeks to gather the facts of their situation, call them with an interim report. Once you have the information, don't waste a lot of time on excuses and explanations. The customer already knows what happened. What they want to know now is what you're going to do about it.

Compensation – if it's possible to redo the work correctly, then do it. In many cases it's impossible to go back and make it right. In these cases, you need to be creative in how you balance things. The customer has paid you money and in their minds did not get their money's worth. While a cash refund may balance the scales financially, it likely will not keep them as a customer. Give them a certificate to be redeemed in the future at your business. This brings them back to do business with you once again. Make sure that when they do return, everything is perfect.

Keep Logs – customer complaints are an immediate indication of problems in your products and services. Keep accurate logs about the types of complaints that you receive to look for trends.

Corrections – once you identify trends, make corrections. The world's most effective Customer Service Program is to eliminate future complaints by changing the way you do things. Address your efforts to the other end of the process – the delivery of products and services. If you have 50 cases of missing luggage, your problem is not better Customer Service procedures.

You may have the best business operation in the universe. You may have the best products, the best services. Your staff may be so well trained that nothing ever slips through the cracks. Yet, one day, something will go wrong and you'll have an unhappy customer. What you do at that juncture will change whether that customer returns to do business with you again in the future or jumps ship to one of your competitors.

Your Customer Service Department is the last checkpoint before your customers defect. Give your Customer Service representatives the tools and guidance they need to keep the customers in the fold.

How to Deliver Bad News

It was one of those things that are funny when happening to someone else, less so when it's your emotions yo-yoing up and down with the alternating delivery.

"Mr. Frank, good news.   We've found the problem."

Our throw all the junk in the back go anywhere 10 year old Trooper is in the car hospital to cure a pathetic shortage of power and constant stalling.

"The fuel and ignition systems all are okay." The mechanic just eliminated with one breath the things that would have been relatively cheap to fix. What was he so happy about?

"So what's wrong?" I timidly query. I had hoped all it needed was new spark plugs.

"The head is cracked." The spark plugs were fine. It was the engine they screwed into that was dying.

"You're kidding. Is that a simple repair?"

"Should be less than $2000 with parts and labor," he said glibly. We can have it done in a week or so."

Washed and waxed on a sunny day with the engine running like a Swiss watch, the poor Trooper might be worth all of $5000 and this fool, eager for the sale, is telling me about a $2000 repair like it's an oil change. Carol and I are clearly going to have one of those agonizing "should we" or "shouldn't we" discussions over supper.

If you provide service to your clients, you are inevitably going to have to break bad news to them from time to time. And you are immediately in a box. Their bad news is your good news. An expensive repair for them means a big sale for you. However, rubbing your hands together as if you've just won the lottery is not the best way to tell the client that the family chariot is terminal.

How do you tell the client they need major repairs in a way that makes the sale for you, maintains the client relationship, and keeps everyone as happy as possible? Here are some pointers that will yield better results along the way:

Soften the blow – Remember the story about the calloused drill sergeant who barked out "Brown your mother died yesterday," in front of the morning formation. While not nearly as serious, you still want to deliver the news in a way that demonstrates you understand how frustrating it is to find a repair they thought was going to be $150 is suddenly $2000. Use your best white-coated physician bedside manner and be consoling.

Give consultation – Suggest alternatives. Help them make the decision whether or not to make the repair. Switch roles from being a salesman to being a friend giving advice. Even though you want them to decide to go forward with the repair, provide alternatives to fixing what's broken.

Offer service contracts – In many industries, you can smooth out the client's cash flow (and yours at the same time) by setting up a service agreement where they pay the same amount every month and you provide repairs as they are needed. This allows them to budget more accurately. It also ensures that next time the machinery rolls over and dies you'll get the repair work.

Prevention is the Best Cure – Are there ways the client could prevent these repairs? Would periodic maintenance have helped? This is a good time to sell a program of more frequent maintenance or a service contract.

Easy payment plans – Offer ways to stretch the financial pain so the client doesn't have to pony up the full amount all at once. Your clients, whether they are individuals or corporations, are typically dealing with daily budget issues. They are seldom prepared for expensive unexpected repairs. Help them make the decision to go forward without destroying their checkbook.

Make the experience positive – Repairs are a zero sum game. When you fix their cars or heat pumps, you only bring them back to zero – the exact point where they were before the machinery went catywhumpus. Give them more than just the repair. Wash their car. Give the machine a complete service. Clean the filters. Give them a box of chocolates. Make the experience as positive and enjoyable as practical given the circumstances.

Don't look to the client for understanding -- You just spent several hours diagnosing their problem and estimating the repair cost and time to complete them. As you rattle this off to the customer, you'll find a marked lack of appreciation for your efforts. This is not the time to expect them to congratulate you. Regardless of how much you've done, they still expect you to sympathize with them.

Whatever industry you are in, your customers are seldom prepared for surprise repairs. Find ways to help them through the rough spots and prevent them in the future. They'll depend on you more, trust you more and give you more business.

What did we decide about the Trooper? We swallowed hard, pulled up our socks, and got the head repaired. That was 2 weeks to the day before the brakes ground themselves into little pieces. The mechanic at the brake place could barely contain his glee as he described the carnage to calipers, rotors, and pads. We decided he was too happy and donated the Trooper to Goodwill.

I sent you a Brochure........

Does this telephone call sound familiar?

"Good morning Mr. Frank.   This is Clyde Emerson, from International Great Products Company. I sent you a brochure on our Great Products last week. Did you get it?"

"No!"

"No? Well that's puzzling. I put it in the mail last Tuesday; you should have received it on Thursday. Are you sure you didn't receive it? It was blue and gold."

"Nope. Don't remember it."

"It had our name in big red letters on the front. Would you mind looking around for it? I'll be glad to wait."

I hung up.

As inane as this scenario reads, you've inevitably received calls just like it. For some reason, following up on a direct mail piece is something sales people routinely massacre. Prospecting callers, peering through the wrong end of the telescope, focus on the mailed brochure rather than the real reason for the call -- making the sale. By looking in the wrong direction, they ruin the entire effort.

Direct mail followed by a phone call is an outstanding way to bring in new customers. Executed well, it is one of the most effective marketing methods available. You target specific prospects, contact them in a warm call environment, and quickly weed out the ones who are not true prospects. Done poorly, it wastes enormous amounts of time and money and annoys the prospects to boot.

So how do you increase the likelihood of sales rather than dial tones when you make the calls? Here are a few hints:

A Little Creativity Please – The mail piece is intended to be an icebreaker and warm up your telephone call. Make your piece stand out. There's no rule that says direct mail has to be a letter or brochure. Be unique. Make it 3 dimensional. Use a puzzle, a packet of seeds, a box of candy. "Mr. Frank, I sent you a Frisbee last week," is a great conversational door opener.

Strong Call to Action – While the main intent of the piece is to warm up the reception when you call, encourage them to call you. Make sure your phone number is clear and easy to find. Test your mail piece by handing it to 3 or 4 people you trust. Ask them to take the action you want the person who receives it to do.

Schedule Mailing and Calling -- Don't mail to your entire list at once. Mail 30 each day. Then one week later call that 30. This creates a routine for you to follow and manages your mail program so if you do strike gold, you can respond in a timely manner.

Tactically Speaking – By sending your mail piece first, you take away an easy objection when you call. They can't get you off the phone by saying, "Send me something." You've already sent them something. By implication, they've lost it. To get you to hang up, they have to think of another excuse. While they're thinking, keep telling them your benefits.

Script it and Rehearse it -- Don't plan on winging it with your natural charm. Write a script and rehearse with a tape recorder. When you play the tape back, if you want to hang up on yourself, keep working. Here is a sample of the type of opening you want to achieve: "Mr. Frank, this is Clyde Emerson, from the Wonderful Trucking Company. I sent you a package last week telling you how to save big money on your shipping costs. I'm calling to follow up and see if you have any questions. How do you ship your products now?"

I'll Bring it to You – If the prospect does suggest you mail them something, be ready with a lighthearted answer, "I did that last week and it didn't make it to your desk. Perhaps I'd better bring it over to you."

Appointment Please – Keep in mind each step of your sales program and close each one appropriately. The mail piece is designed to peak interest, call you if possible, and to increase reception when you call them. The follow-up call is to build rapport, to establish whether they are a true prospect and if they are, to schedule an appointment for a sales presentation.

Benefits, Benefits, Benefits – People will buy from you for one reason and one reason only: they see the benefits of doing so. Start by outlining the benefits in your direct mail piece. Continue emphasizing the benefits when you call. Remind them of the benefits when you make the appointment to come and see them.

Direct mail followed by a phone call can be very successful when planned and executed as an entire project. Design the piece as an icebreaker. Make your call enjoyable and productive. When you call, concentrate on the reasons they should buy from you, not the piece you mailed them. Turn your telescope around and look through the right end – at the sale down the road.

I have to go now, the phone is ringing and I still haven't gotten through the mail.

The World's Greatest Salesman

I live next door to one of the world's greatest salesman. His name is Tyler Watkins. He is a great inspiration to me. Tyler smoothly implements every professional sales technique known and tosses in a few that he's developed on his own. He very carefully prepares for each sales presentation, studies his prospect carefully so he is ready to overcome objections, refuses to take no for an answer, and continues working with the prospect until they buy. Tyler has a sales close ratio that would be the envy of anyone in professional sales.

Tyler is 8 years old.

I watched Tyler in action the other day while I was visiting the Watkins house. Tyler came in to the kitchen to make a big sale. "Mom, can I stay up till 9:30 and watch TV? There's a special show on about turtles. My science teacher told us about it."

"No, Tyler. Not tonight," answered his mother, Patty.

"Why not?" asked Tyler immediately.

Note that in 30 seconds Tyler has made his presentation, closed, and is now identifying objections. His mother, the prospect, obediently starts listing them for him.

"Because I want you in bed early and your room is a mess," answers Patty in the mistaken belief that strong objections will discourage the little salesman and he'll go away.

Tyler, undaunted, perseveres and starts selling the benefits. "Mom, I need to see this to help me in science. You want me to get better grades don't you?"

"Of course I want you to get better grades. This will help you get better grades?"

Tyler transitions from salesman to consultant and starts objectively discussing the wisdom of the purchase with the prospect. "Absolutely mom. It's all about where turtles live, how they eat, and how long they live. We're studying about it right now in science. I'll be the star of my class."

"What about your room?" asks Patty as she suddenly remembers her other objection.

"If I clean my room, can I stay up?"

"Yes, all right. But I need to inspect it first," answers Patty to Tyler's back side as he dove into his room. Tyler has just traded something he was supposed to do anyway, clean his room, for the sale.

Every child is by instinct a great salesman. They were born with all the right attributes and they use them beautifully. You can learn more about selling by watching an eight year old than by listening to all the sales motivational tapes on the planet. Here is a list of successful sales traits you can learn from a child:

They won't take "No" for an answer – When the prospect says no, the typical salesperson packs up the briefcase and heads back to the office. A child thinks "No" is the starting gun. They roll up their sleeves, spit on their palms, and start the heavy work of changing the prospect's decision. They truly think if they didn't have a few "No's" to overcome, it would take the fun out of it.

They identify objections – Children are expert at identifying objections. They look you right in the eye and ask why you aren't buying. It's very effective. Then they keep working on you until they have identified every objection and countered it.

They overcome objections – They know that the sale will not be made until each objection has been answered and put away. Once they have identified an objection, they provide a solution.

They're prepared – Children have their sales pitch prepared. They've already role played in their mind their opening presentation and a few responses to objections. When was the last time you roll played a sales scenario in your mind before actually facing the prospect?

They offer benefits – Children instinctively understand the direct relationship between benefits and the decision to purchase. In order to make the sale, they have to make it attractive to their prospect. They not only list the benefits, they do so in a way that prospects realize what a great opportunity this will be for them.

They switch to consultant – Transitioning from salesperson to consultant is a great plus in every sales situation. It is the moment when you come around the desk and sit with them to help them make the right purchase decision. When you accomplish this, prospects no longer have their guard up to defend against the sale. Now they look to you for guidance in helping make a purchase.

They trade things they should have done anyway – Human nature is that everyone wants a little extra. "If we gave you free shipping, would you agree to the order?" may be a very effective way to close the sale. Find ways to emphasize features and benefits to the prospect even if they were there all along. It adds value to your products and makes agreeing to the sale easier. If you're sitting in front of a prospect and are puzzling over how to proceed, remember Tyler offering to clean his room.

They do it with good humor – Children know the advantage of a quick smile. They make you enjoy the process of being sold to by them. No one ever buys from someone they don't like. Make your interaction with your prospects and clients fun, enjoyable, and interesting.

They keep closing – No child stops closing after the first "No." They keep going long after that – until the prospect says "Yes."

Want a quick lesson in sales. Follow an 8-year-old around for a few days. You'll learn more about sales presentations, identifying objections, and closing than you will from a hundred sales training courses. And you'll have a lot more fun.

I have to run now, I promised to take Tyler to the movies. He only had to ask me once; I already knew it would be hopeless to say "No."

When to Start Closing

You're sitting at your desk when the flag goes up. A prospect calls and asks for a demo. With the sales siren blaring in the background, you leap into action. Set the meeting and hang up. Tailor the Power Point presentation. Load the company brochures. Pack product samples. Rehearse your lines. Spiff into your best suit. You're ready to win the customer on the sales battlefield. As you charge out of the garage and gun your way to the prospect meeting, a recurring question tickles at the edges of your mind. When should you start closing?

Most salespeople, however proficient they are at making presentations, aren't great at closing. They close too early. They wait too late. They miss the prospect's blatant buy signals because they are too busy rattling on about their product features. They soften the close with warm fuzzys to avoid putting the client on the spot. Or worst of all, they never close at all and hope their sales presentation was so convincing, the client will sign up on their own.

The main reason most people have trouble closing is their childhood training. Blurting "Can I have a cookie?" as you stormed into Aunt Bertha's living room guaranteed a reprimand in the car on the way home.

Politeness was hammered into us from when we learned to tell time and selling goes directly uphill against those youthful lessons. It's hardly gracious manners to look someone directly in the eye and say, "Sign here."

An added obstacle for most professionals is that they consider it completely beneath them to ask for the sale. No one goes to law school for 3 years so they can reduce themselves to begging the client to do business with them. Or do they?

Welcome to business. You're now in an environment where NOT asking for the cookie can cost big time. If your sales presentation is outstanding but your competitor is the one that asks for the order, the competitor will get the business. It doesn't matter if you are a law firm or an office supply company. Selling is the same for everyone.

So here you are, on the way to meet the prospect. When do you start closing? Here's an answer that will change the way you look at the entire selling process. Start closing the second you arrive. Forget wondering when it is the right time. It's as you get out of the car. Start evaluating the client and weaving what you know about them into your sales presentation from the start. Here's how you do it:

Image – What does their facility look like? Match your presentation to the image they project. If they are a first rate operation, you can start heading off price objections now by reminding them that they aren't the kind of company that travels in steerage.

Accoutrements – What do they have pasted on their walls? Are they into sports, art, ballet? Use these observations to appeal to their emotions: "A company with your rich culture will be sure to appreciate the quality of our products."

Goals – The most critical element of their decision to buy from you will be your proving that your products meet their goals. You can't prove you can help them meet their goals if you don't know their goals. Before you start babbling about your product features, ask pertinent questions about the benefits they expect to receive. Build their goals into everything you do, say, or present. "This new sign will be a significant contribution to reaching your increased revenue goals next year, Mr. Frank."

Decision Makers – Who will be making the purchase decision? Don't waste your time trying to close someone who can't even decide to go with you. Find the right person before the presentation and present to them as well. If you can't find or be in front of the decision maker, close the person you can reach on selling you and your company to the decision maker. An advocate inside their company is critical.

What Next? – Make the steps to do business with you crystal clear. Spell out what to do next and provide them with everything they need to begin. If you want them to sign a contract, give it to them and hand them the pen.

Ask for the Order – There are many professional, non-insulting ways to ask for the order. Use them. Rehearse various close techniques in the privacy of your own office so you don't fumble your way through this in public. Use direct questions. Did we meet your goals? Does our product match your corporate image? Is this price what you had in mind? What do we need to do to go forward? Are you ready to move forward?

Closing is the most vital element of your whole sales program. Without it, you've wasted all the time you invested in making the presentation. Start closing the second you meet the prospect and continue until they sign, even if it means looking them in the eye and asking for the order.

But it's still not a great idea to ask for a cookie when your mom takes you to visit her neighbors.

Accounting As An Advertising Strategy?

How important is accounting to your advertising?

That's right, accounting. I know, I know, a marketing book should be providing creative ideas on clever advertising campaigns possibly featuring a winsome gopher named Ralph who sings a witty jingle with such a catchy tune that people will soon be singing it in their daily shower. Accounting is, well, just accounting. It has nothing to do with marketing.

Or does it?

Accounting, or rather a comprehensive data flow about your clients, is an absolute essential to monitor the success of any marketing program. More critical, it provides you with the information to tailor your advertising and increase its cost effectiveness. By correctly designing the software system that logs in new business, you will have an ongoing information stream to tell you whether your singing gopher is doing his job.

Depending on your business, you want to make up a list of the information about each client and each prospect that will help you define and refine your client universe. The basics are pretty straightforward:

- Name

- Address

- Zip code

- Telephone number

- Email address

You may also want to add:

- Age bracket

- Income bracket

- Profession

Then you'll want several informational items specific to your industry. For example, if you are in auto sales, you might want:

- Current auto

- Auto looked at

- Referred by

Gathering this information is typically a combination of discipline and sales strategy. Virtually everyone will give you basic name, address and phone number. Age, income, and possibly profession could fall into the intrusive category and will be difficult to gather unless asked for correctly. People will typically give answers to these questions if they are posed on a written form with multiple choice answers. For example, give several age brackets and income brackets. Some people, of course, still will not want to provide that information and will leave those items blank on your form. Even so, the information from the people who will provide it will be valuable.

Once you've gone to the trouble to gather information and enter it into the computer, what do you do with it? First let's look at the advertising strategy.

The age, income, and profession information will provide you with specific demographics of your client base. For example, if a significant portion of customers are engineers, consider advertising in engineering publications. If there is a large contingent of customers over 60 years old, look into senior citizen publications. Establishing customer profiles will also help you do a better job of serving them. For example if a significant number are in their 20's and 30's, look into providing child care.

Do data runs on the types of items brought in for service. Look for trends. For example, if a large number of 3–5 year old Chevrolets are being traded in at your auto dealership, a very cost effective advertising program could be direct mail to 3-5 year old Chevrolet owners. This reaches exactly your target audience without wasting marketing funds on people who are less likely to be potential customers.

With this information logged into your computer, you can also generate critical management reports. Here are the ones you want to see every week:

- Revenues this week compared to 1 and 2 weeks ago.

- How many potential clients came in compared to how many bought (close ratio).

- Work in progress.

Revenue trends are, of course, critical management information. They will alert you before problems hit the bottom line. The close ratio is one of your most dramatic ways of increasing your bottom line. These are people standing in your business ready to do business with you. If you've gone to the trouble of giving them an estimate or proposal, you've already done all of the marketing work. Now close the sale. Look for ways to increase the percentage of closes to people who have made it through the estimate or proposal stage. A 10% change here is worth far, far more than a 10% return on your advertising. Do the math, you'll be amazed.

A singing gopher named Ralph may very well help your business generate leads. But put this system in place first so you can use the information wisely when those leads come through your door.

Safe at Second

Marketing Tip #37 – Learn from others selling to you.

I needed to hire someone. I called two companies who provide the type of service needed and set a meeting with each. I outlined project, goals, and expectations. I asked for a proposal.

Company A faxed a form proposal of a few success stories and their services price list. Company B brought bells and whistles. They proudly presented a detailed program of how they would achieve my specific goals. It included research results, vendor costs, time line, even creative spec artwork. They brought the whole enterprise in at exactly our budget. Needless to say, we hired Company B.

Now this could easily be about proposal skills, but it's not. It's about what followed my announcement of the winner.

Company A, who came in second for a project they should have won, had a choice of several marketing tactics. They chose the worst option possible. They torched the bridge.

The president of Company A, who apparently never mastered rejection as a child, sent me a blistering letter. Included in his diatribe were such gems as: the fault lay at my feet; I didn't specifically ask them to be creative in their proposal; and they never give away labor for free. He concluded by stating they had already decided not to work with me because I did not return their phone calls for 3 days. He should reread Aesop's Fox and Grapes. In a fit of overreaction, this man categorically ensured that his company will never get my business, regardless of whether Company B lives up to their glowing promises.

Any time two or more companies bid for a job, one or more will lose out. That's simple math. What are you going to do when you learn that you spent all that energy preparing your proposal and you aren't the one going to the altar? How do you handle coming in second?

Hopefully you deal with rejection more graciously than Company A does. But, as much as anyone hates to lose, you should have a program in place to make the most of it when it happens. Here's how to lose the battle but win the war:

Don't Get Personal – Selling is a competition, not an individual affront. Instead of calling your analyst – consider this setback as if you were playing Chess and your opponent took your Queen – it hurts but it's not the end of the game. Start planning your next move.

Use Courtesy as a Sales Tool – When you get the news, respond with all the professionalism you can muster. This is the time to cement a future relationship – do it by impressing them with your business demeanor.

Learn from Mistakes – What put your competitor out in front? Your prospect will tell you. In fact they'll likely tell you the elements of the winning proposal and the price as well. Ask them. You need to know why you lost! Vowing to work harder next time won't deliver better results if you have a fatal flaw in your presentation or pricing. Learn it now.

Keep the Bridge – Call the prospect 2 – 3 weeks later. Now that you're not trying to sell them something, be a friend and consultant. Establish that they actually did sign with your competitor. A lot can happen between proposal and contract. If anything went awry, you want to know about it. You're available if they need a replacement.

Until Death do We Part – Business is a progression, not an event. Start selling for next time. Call them every couple months. Offer assistance and advice. Stay with them. You'll be the first one they call at the next go around.

The Secret of Success – Here's a closely guarded secret. If they received 10 proposals, you'll be the only one of 9 losers who stays in touch. In fact, you're likely the only one of the entire 10 contenders. Winning salesmen never call either – they're too busy looking for new business. The next time the prospect needs your services, guess who has the inside track?

No one enjoys rejection. But dealing with it as a professional can lead to a successful sale down the road and referrals along the way. Don't burn the bridge. Use it to cross over to the prospect again.

Take No Prisoners

Marketing is a complex process of strategy, sales, collateral materials, advertising, and presentations. Yet, if you were asked to reduce the entire process of marketing into one short sentence, what would you say?

My answer will not only change your perspective, but using it will dramatically improve your results. Here's the *Marketing Guy's* definition of successful marketing: Take business away from your competition!

It's that simple. In order for you to win, your competitors have to lose. If your industry writes proposals before making the sale, being awarded the contract very clearly means beating out other contenders. If you are in retail, the battle lines may not be as obvious, but they are no less definitive. They have to lose for you to win.

Once you start looking at the marketing process as a competitive battle, you see it differently. Your see it as a combative process and fight your competition for every sale and for every customer. However, before you call your competitors and arrange to meet at dawn with drawn pistols, let's discuss a few more business like methods of fighting. Then you can decide if pistols are still your best option.

The first step of preparing a battle plan is to assemble the right weapons. Here are the basics:

Know thy enemy -- The first advantage in any campaign is a comprehensive understanding of the strengths and weaknesses of your enemy. Shop your competitors. Identify what they do poorly and make sure your company does it better. Note everything they do well and confirm that your company does these substantially better. Make a list of every advantage that your company has over your competition, every feature you offer they don't, every service, every product.

Know your customers – The next step is to completely understand your customers and their buying triggers. Survey your customers to learn why they choose you over your competition. What advantages do they see in doing business with you? What advantages do they find in doing business with your competitors? How do they make the decision which company to buy from?

Know yourself – This sounds crazy, but most managers don't know their own business well enough. Now that you've shopped your competition and talked to your customers, shop yourself. Go ahead, try to buy something from your company. If you can't do this personally, hire someone to come in and do it. Be as critical as your most demanding customer. Compare your company with your competition. If there are any areas where you are weak, fix them. Highlight your strengths and improve on them. Make sure shopping with your company is truly more enjoyable than it is at the competition.

Once you have done the research, put together a *Plan de Combat.* Here's how to create a strategy to take their customers away from them:

Go for their weaknesses – Feature things you do better in your ads and sales presentations. You can highlight their weaknesses by emphasizing your strengths. For example, if your competitors typically don't train their sales people very well, boast "Staffed by professional consultants" for your company.

Go them one better – If your competitors provide delivery, offer training as well. Then build that entire package into your sales presentation. "Where others only offer delivery, we provide the training you need to quickly benefit from our products." Prospective customers are looking for reasons to buy from you. Give them many.

Build an Invincible Army – Arm your entire sales staff with comprehensive knowledge about the competition. Their bullets are all the ways you are better. Rehearse possible objections to and effective rebuttals. Build all you know about the competition into your sales presentations, knocking them subtly and accurately without compromising your professional standards. Do it by highlighting your strengths and referring obliquely to general weaknesses of other companies. For example, "Our customers told us they had difficulty in getting service. We have a 24 hour hot line staffed with experts who are ready to help you when you need it."

Espirit de Corps – Motivate your team to win. Develop a campaign slogan. Buy T-shirts. Hold sales meetings to discuss battle plans. Hold contests. Drum into your sales staff that winning on your side equals losing for the other side. They must take the customers away from your competition. Make sure they know every day that they are going into battle – a sales battle for the customer.

Marketing means winning customers away from the competition. Start thinking of marketing this way and you immediately have a different perspective. Start doing marketing this way and you immediately have better results.

On the other hand, there are always pistols.

Know Thy Customer

Do you know your customers? I'll bet you don't. I'll even go so far as to wager that you can't successfully answer 5 basic questions about them. If you can truthfully explain a few critical elements about your customers and how they do business with you, call me. I'll admit I'm wrong, something that doesn't happen too often, and take you to lunch. Here are the questions. Write down your answers, then call your clients and check your answers.

1. What benefits do your customers get from buying your products and services (their answer, not yours)?

2. Why do they buy from you rather than the competition?

3. What additional services would they buy from you if you offered them?

4. What percentage of you customers haven't bought from you for over 6 months?

5. Describe the demographics of your customers (Size, age, location, industry, etc.)

6. Bonus Question -- What do your customers like best about your products or services?

How did you do? Am I stuck for lunch?

Likely not. Most managers don't know their customers. Yet, knowing how your customers shop with you is critical to your success. If you don't understand your customers and their buying triggers, you are making vital management decisions in the dark. Worse, you are wasting much of your marketing budget by advertising in the wrong places with themes that don't match client buying triggers.

One of the most effective marketing actions you can ever take is to survey your own customers. This must be done in person, either over the phone or face to face. Mail surveys won't cut it for this kind of project. Customers are unlikely to take the time and effort to complete and return questionnaires with the information you need. Start the project by doing the following:

1. Assign people to do the survey. These can be managers, sales people, or an outside firm who will bring a disinterested perspective. Whoever it is, they must be professional, courteous, and very good listeners.

2. Create a written script. This should include: an introduction, the question, "Is this a good time to talk?" and an explanation of why you are calling.

3. Empower your interviewers to solve customer problems. You will unquestionably find problems; solve them now and gain a customer for life. If the interviewers are not staff members of the company, they can solve customer problems by promising to have someone call tomorrow.

4. Establish a method of recording customer responses. The easiest way to do this is to print a questionnaire with the introduction script on the top. Then use one copy for each interview. Write answers after the questions as you talk to each

client. Alternatively, tape record the conversations
– be sure to ask the client first.

5. Make a management commitment to listen to the
results and implement operational adjustments as
needed. This sounds silly at this stage, but do it
anyway. You are going to hear a lot of things
about your company. Some you may not want to
hear. Do it anyway. If you customers tell you
something about your company that you don't
think is true, who do you think is right?

When you're done with the interviews, compile the
results. You'll have in your hand next year's marketing
and management plan. Additional services or products
you should be offering are clearly spelled out by the
people most capable of making those decisions – the
people who will buy them. Management changes you
should implement are the answers to the questions:
"What do you like least?" "What could we improve?" and
"What would you tell our president?"

You'll find a theme for your advertising too – it's
how clients use your products and why they choose you
over your competition. For example, if they say they like
doing business with you because they can get right
through, launch an advertising campaign based on the
theme, "No Voice Mail – talk to a real person." The
demographics on your customers combined with their
reading/listening preferences tell you exactly where to
advertise to reach them.

On top of having your marketing plan written for
you, you'll receive a bonus benefit from this project. Your
customers will think much more of you because you took
the time to ask them their opinions. The survey itself is
actually a pretty clever marketing technique. Just doing it
will increase sales.

So get going and meet your customers. They'll enjoy hearing from you and you'll enjoy hearing from them. Tell them hello from me.

Need Help?
Look in the Appendix for a Sample Customer Interview Form.

How to Read a Newspaper

A quick saunter through any newspaper and you're left with the impression that half of the companies in the county have just invented some thingytwirler that will significantly make the world a better place or signed a new contract that will increase their revenues by a zillion fold. The other half have all hired new personnel. From trade publications to general media newspapers, all are chock full of names and accomplishments.

The correct technical term for these news articles is: Sales Leads. That's right you can use this information to sell to the people and companies highlighted. But how do you leap the chasm between learning that *Advanced Computer Stuff* just invented software to automatically read bedtime stories to 3 year olds and selling that company on using your coffee service, especially when every one of your competitors heard the same starting gun you did. Do you dive for the phone, hoping to nail the prospect before the competition shows up? Should you send a letter, flowers, a congratulatory card? How about popping over and strolling into their office?

While there are no assurances that any system, from flowers to surprise visits, will yield the sale, here is one absolute guarantee. Doing nothing more than saying to yourself, "This person is a good sales lead," will not ring the cash register. In sales, as in life itself, there is very strong connectivity between actions and results. So what actions can you take that will create the sales results you want?

From promotions to new inventions, people like to know that someone saw their name in print. By professionally congratulating them on their accomplishments you can move into discussing your products and service and their needs. Here are a few techniques that will work to create sales from news articles.

First the homework:

Cut the Chaff – Who are your ideal customers? What size business do you serve best? What industry? Cull through the names overflowing from the newspaper and identify your true potential clients. Don't waste time on the chaff – aim for the wheat.

Why Do Business with You? – What benefits will customers receive from using your products and services. Have a list ready to write letters, start conversations, and stir up interest.

Use the Magic Box – If you don't have a computerized contact management system, get one now. This is the most critical tool to making any sales campaign a success. Your system must merge letters, print labels, and sort by category (industry, location, size, etc.) Create fields that will hold accomplishments as well as publication name and date.

Now get your selling tools ready:

Epistles to Go -- Write an interesting form letter. Start with congratulating them on their good news. Finish by showing how they could be even more successful by using your products and services.

Hello, How are You? -- Write a script for follow-up phone calls. This is an easy call -- you have something to congratulate them about.   Move smoothly into a discussion of how your products and services will be of benefit to them.   Do NOT start the call by asking, "How are you?"

At the Beep -- Don't be surprised when you get their Voice Mail -- you are going to be relegated to the recorder more often than finding a real person at their desk. Prepare now to deal with it in a way that leads to the sale – write a script! Make your message lively and fun – stand out from the 53 other Voice Mails they waded through when they returned.

Go Into the Closet – Check your supply of brochures and collateral materials. When you stir up enough interest for them to ask for more information, be ready with the materials.

Now you're ready to start. Using the color of your choice, highlight every article that contains a viable sales lead for your company – throw away the rest.   Once a week, enter the leads into your computer. Personalize and generate the letters, then mail them out.   Call each prospect one week after you mail the letter. Allocate time on your schedule every week for entry, mailing, and follow-up phone calls.

Keep prospects on your mailing list. Make sure they see something from your company (letter, newsletter, post card, Frisbee) every 6 weeks or so. If they don't have the sense to buy from you right away, wear them down with direct mail.

This   system   will   increase   your   network   of prospects, build your mailing list, and ultimately result in more sales. You're paying for the publications that pile up in your In Box every week – make them pay you back through increased revenues. However, before you wander

through the newspaper in search of sales leads, read the
Marketing Guy Column first.

Who is your customer?

My sister, Sandy Cooper, has two Masters Degrees and is principal of an elementary school. She makes over $60,000 a year and has 85 employees. 1500 students call her Mrs. Cooper. She recently ambled into an auto dealership to buy a new car. The salesman told her to come back with her husband.

The tragedy of this is not just that someone was picking on my little sister, but that an auto dealership who probably spent 200 advertising dollars to bring each prospective customer through their door, lost the sale with an unthinking act by a chauvinistic salesman. Guess how many of Sandy's teachers and staff heard this story? They're not shopping at that dealership now either. The dealership's cost per prospect through the door just skyrocketed upwards!

How do you prevent this kind of catastrophe in your business? You invest all that money in advertising to bring prospects in the front door. You cannot afford to have them walk back out without buying something. Women account for more and more purchasing decisions both in families and on their own. Yet there is a lingering philosophy that a woman alone cannot make a significant purchase commitment, such as buying an automobile, without her male counterpart. If your company is operating under this mythology, you are sending a large number of sales directly to the competition.

This might be a good time to develop a training program for your sales staff. Here are a few things to include:

Respect – you don't need an Affirmative Action program to appreciate that all customers want to be treated with respect. Ensuring that staff members carry out the company respect program is admittedly a challenge. I have found that companies that treat each other with respect do a better job of respecting their customers. Work on programs that raise your Respect Quotient across the board.

Getting to Know You – Does your sales staff know their prospects? Understanding the client is the key to sales success. Knowing the needs and expected benefits of each client prospect is critical to making the sale. Have sales people describe prospects after they leave your store including hobbies, family, and how they will use your products. This forces sales people to get to know their prospects, if for no other reason than to be able to answer your questions afterwards.

Judging a Book by its Cover – There are thousands of examples of sales lost from misjudging the prospect's ability to buy. Perhaps the most famous example is when the president of Harvard ignored a couple who wanted to make a gift to the college in honor of their son who died. The college president was irritated that this poor looking couple was taking up his valuable time. He insulted them because they looked so shabby. As a result, they invested their $7 million to start Stanford University rather than make the gift to Harvard. Do not let your sales staff decide who should be a customer by appearance. Don't let them make those decisions based on race, gender, or shoe size either.

Who Lost the Sale – Demand an explanation whenever a prospect leaves without buying. Explaining exactly what the prospect came in for and why they didn't purchase is an excellent tool to prevent lost sales through inept sales tactics. "They were just looking," is not an acceptable answer.

Management -- A good sales manager should know the prejudices of his sales people. Keep track of trends. I would have a serious talk with any sales person who had not sold to single women.

Allocate Your Resources – Acknowledge that some people are better in certain situations than others. Designate people to wait on particular customer groups. This is by no means discriminatory, it's smart business. Assign the sales staff where they have the best chance of closing.

Ask any woman if she's ever felt discriminated against and stand back for the onslaught of stories. This happens so frequently that, unless you own a dress store, take for granted it happens in your business. Customers come in all sizes, shapes, colors, and genders. To be successful, you have to sell to them all, whether they be women, people who wear yellow hats, or families of 4. Once you get a prospect in the door, sell to them whoever they are.

Especially if they happen to be a school principal with access to a PA system.

The Business Prevention Department

Do you have a Business Prevention Department? That's a group of people in your company who prevent business from happening.

You don't think you do?   Read the following example and tell me if the same thing could happen in your company. This example is completely true and I am reporting it exactly as it happened.   Since this story is critical of the company involved, I have gone to great lengths to protect their identity.

A few years ago, Carol and I bought a new boat. The boat had a TV and DVD so I decided to buy a video library. I pictured watching videos and munching popcorn while anchored in some peaceful cove. I went to that full color ad on the back of the Sunday magazine section and ordered a whole slew of videos.   This automatically enrolled me in the "Club" and "allowed" me to choose a video each month from their colorful, enticing catalogue.

This worked pretty well for a while. They sent us videos, we sent them money. The "Club" and I were both reasonably happy with relationship.   One day I ordered 3 videos. However instead of filling my order, the "Club" sent me a notice that I owed them $12.63. They refused to send any more videos until I paid up.

I sent them a blistering letter telling them I didn't owe them any money and they'd better send my videos. They sent a form letter telling me to pay up. This went back and forth a couple times, me penning furious (but very creative) letters dripping with sarcasm, their return form letters consisting of one repeated message, pay the $12.63. I finally admitted defeat, sent them a check for $12.63, and cancelled my membership. The video collection was about to sink the boat anyway.

A month later I received a letter from the "Club" telling me I had overpaid my account by $12.63. They sent me a check for, $12.63.

This story is funny unless you happen to be the company in question, in which case it's tragic. I'm willing to bet that no one in their advertising department knows this story. The company spends all that money for full color ads in the Sunday supplements. They devote their energies to bringing new customers in through the front door. All the while, their credit department is chasing them out the back door with inept accounting procedures. Do you think "the Club's" marketing department thinks their company has a Business Prevention Department? I bet not. Yet, we'd still be loading down the boat with videos if it hadn't been for the accounting mishap.

When it comes to planning a marketing strategy, the credit department typically isn't even on the landscape. After all, they're over there doing accounting and boring stuff having nothing to do with sales. Or do they? Do your credit department and marketing department talk? More critical, do you have procedures in place so when a customer does owe you money, you collect it without killing the relationship?

To make sure you don't have a Business Prevention Department, here are some procedures to consider:

1. Review everything the credit department sends to the client, from invoices to past due letters and make sure they are consistent with the image you want your company to convey. Be sure your phone number is on your invoice so customers can call if they have any questions. Encourage them to do so if they have a problem.

2. When a customer is late on a payment, involve the salesperson in collection. The sales staff has a vested interest in keeping the customer as well as making sure payment happens. The credit department too often concentrates on the "pay" part and ignores the "keep the customer" part.

3. Late or non-payment very often is a result of a problem the customer had with the order. Call customers soon after delivery to make sure everything is satisfactory. Don't wait until the customer is 60 days late to find out they didn't get what they ordered.

4. Send your credit department to a sales training course. They are as much part of the marketing team as the sales staff – make sure they know it.

5. When a customer cancels or leaves you, make sure you know the true reason why. When you find trends, make changes to ensure your company's actions are never a cause of losing a customer.

You don't need a Business Prevention Department – you worked too hard to get the customer in the first place. Work to make sure every experience they have with you is pleasant and enjoyable. Keep them coming back forever.

And come and go boating with us some day.   Do you have any recent videos you can bring along?

Give Free Time

After receiving a cellular bill roughly the size of Albania's national budget, I decided it was time to change phone companies. Rather than follow our last system for choosing a cellular company, signing up at the electronics store while we were buying speakers, I decided to do actual research this time.

This is not easy. You need at a minimum the Yellow Pages, a calculator, your past cell phone bill, a large legal pad, and a great deal of patience. Pen in hand, I started dialing and asked each cellular vendor how they could improve my life. Virtually every one is giving away something "Free" to entice you to do business with them. One has free weekend air time, the other has free minutes. Another has free evenings and weekends, but it was only until the year 2000. Since the entire system was likely to crash over Y2K, that would not be good enough.

After writing down each cellular company's rates, I created a sample bill for my usage with each service including the "Free" Stuff. The result, happily, was a company who would reduce the monthly cell bills to, if not reasonable, at least bearable levels. My mother might actually hear from me more than quarterly.

To save time, I faxed the phone application back to them. They called to say everything was approved and I set an appointment to pick up the new phone. There appears to be a strict rule in the cell phone industry that they cannot charge or activate a cell phone unless the customer is standing at the counter. In fact, they apparently can't even get it out of the box until you are standing there.

All in all, it took nearly an hour before mom or anyone else could receive a cellular call from me. The new phone went belly up the next morning so it was back to the vendor where we went through the whole opening box, charging, activating routine all over again. More hours down the drain.

As companies fall all over themselves to give something away "free" to drag in new customers, I wonder why they squander so freely the one thing consumers value so dearly, TIME. An excellent way to stand out from your competition is to make purchasing from you less time consuming. One of the most valuable freebies you can give your customers is their own time. If you invest the effort to find ways to reduce the time required to buy from your company, you will find a large increase in sales with no increased expense.

Here are some hints to giving more "Free" customer time:

Free Delivery – Dominos revolutionized the pizza industry with free delivery, not better pizza. Are there ways you can bring your products to the customer so they can save the time of coming to your store? Imagine how many customers I would have referred to my cell phone store if they had brought the phone to me?

Please enter the last name, social security number, and department of the person you are calling, then press the pound sign -- What obstacles are between your customers and an order? Finding your phone number? Voice Mail? A receptionist who doesn't know where to direct the call? Waiting on hold? Unless you are a tech support department, where people expect to stay on hold for at least 2 days, you want to make the process of connecting with your order department as smooth and as FAST as possible. Don't make people jump through hoops to reach you.

Check Please – We once bought a bunch of living room stuff at a furniture store. Carol and I wandered around the store selecting knick-knacks, mirrors, a wall unit. When we finished making our selections, we attempted to pay and head on to other errands. I say attempted because they kept us waiting for 30 minutes while they laboriously entered each item into their computer to calculate the invoice. Then they realized they forgot to charge us for one $25 item and started the whole process over again, even though our bill was over $1000. The next year when we bought a whole new living room, guess who didn't get our business? Customers consider all the time they spend shopping to be time well spent. As soon as they are done, they expect you to complete your part of the transaction with minimal time cost to them. Make sure your "check out" procedures are as smooth and efficient as possible.

Service R Us – Twice a year (birthday and Christmas) I head for Nordstrom's with Carol's size written on a sticky note. The minute I hit the women's department a salesperson starts showing me what will fit. This means I get in and out in minutes and since I'm far more likely to hit it right on the first go, the return factor is significantly lower as well. It saves a great deal of time on both sides, not to mention aggravation. What ways can you find to speed up the process of selection at your business?

Fast Means Now – McDonalds started a whole industry with the simple premise of having the food ready when the customer came through the door. Can you have your products ready when customers come in the door?

Every one of your customers, regardless of who they are or what industry you are in, wishes they had more time. Your customers are already torn between attending their daughter's field hockey game, picking up the dry cleaning and finishing the Acme proposal. In deciding whether to shop with you, they consider whether it is worth the trouble. Picture the last time you decided not to buy something because it was too much trouble. Then think about what the business could have done to make it easier to shop there. Do the same thing to your business.

But the contract said............

During a momentary lapse of judgment a while back, I agreed to chair the website committee for our Rotary Club. This had all the earmarks of a pain in the neck project: getting a committee to agree on something as extensive as a website design, explaining the website to older club members who wondered what you meant by "online," negotiating a contract between a vendor and a non-profit group. Still, I was brave and hearty and figured I had the experience and expertise to oversee the project. I planned to bring happiness and light to the hearts of all our Rotary members. Have you ever noticed that's the feeling you have right before a calamity?

During the courtship, the vendor we ultimately selected was all peaches and rosebuds. They promised a website that we would proudly show the world. They promised a team relationship. They wanted every member of Rotary to see what a great job they did and thus recommend them. They promised cookies and ice cream at our meetings. We were in love.

However, a funny thing happened between the courtship and delivery. Not only did we not get the cookies and ice cream; the resultant website was a far cry from what we had envisioned. So much for my expertise and experience preventing dismay in Mudville. When I attempted to outline our concerns to the vendor they responded with a terse, "Well, we fulfilled everything in our contract." Apparently there was no joy in Vendor-ville either.

Has this ever happened in your business? You think you have delivered all that was agreed on and the customer still wants more. Both sides are dialing their attorneys at the very time you should be breaking out the drinks. Next comes mud slinging over terms and often a parting of ways.

As a manager, you need to consider examples like this one, explore what went wrong, and determine how to prevent similar occurrences in your own business. You want to establish procedures that allow you to bubble in champagne rather than bristle at attorneys at the project conclusion.

Here are some ways to prevent a battle with your customer at the end of the project:

Set Expectations Accurately – The primary cause of unhappiness at delivery is mismatched expectations. The sales department, in their enthusiasm for getting the sale, typically promises the moon. The production department delivers something a whole lot more earthy. The contract should capture everything that has been promised and is expected by the customer. In the sales presentation, our Rotary Club was promised 3 versions of a design to choose from before the site was constructed. No one (including yours truly, Mr. Experience) noticed that this was conveniently left out of the contract. We only received one version. Although the agreement did not include it, we still expected 3 versions to choose from. When the agreement is crafted, go over it with the customer and ask them if there were any expectations that were not covered in the written document.

Communicate During Production – Bring the client in while the product is developed. Get their approval at critical stages of the creation process so when the final product is completed, it matches what they agreed to all along. During production, if you have any problems, explain these issues to the client immediately. Clients can deal with anything better than they can deal with surprises. Our Rotary Club was given one photocopy of a proposed layout at the beginning and then presented with the final completed site with no conversation in between. This kind of "working in the dark" will inevitably lead to disappointments.

Record Change Orders – Another sure formula for unhappiness is to present a bill for significantly more than the contract. After the fact pointing out of requested changes does NOT soften a budget-busting invoice. Make sure the production department has a copy of the agreement and they are very clear on the specific deliverables of the contract. When a request is outside the agreement, write up a change order, estimate the cost of the change, and have the client sign it. At the end of the project you both know what to expect.

Deliver with Excitement – This is a special occasion – you've finished the product they ordered. Make the delivery special. Bring in a marching band. Serve cookies and ice cream. Make it a celebration. While you have their attention, demonstrate their new product and explain how it works. Frequently dissatisfaction comes more from a lack of understanding than from a true unhappiness with the product.

The Client Didn't Buy a Contract -- Remember the customer paid little or no attention to the agreement. Our Rotary Club had to scramble to find which member even had the agreement before we could compare it to the final product. Clients purchase the product they envision, not the one described in the contract. It is your job to deliver to that image. While both sides need a written agreement to capture the essence of the work arrangement, remember the client is buying something to serve a need, not a 3-page contract.

Keeping your current clients happy is one of the most dramatic marketing accomplishments you can make. If they are unhappy, they refuse to pay. Ultimately you lose the revenues from the sale or worse, end up in court. Keeping them happy throughout the production and delivery process is far easier and less painful.

So what happened with the Rotary Club Website? We argued with the vendor until we both grew tired of the process. The Club decided to swallow our losses and find a new supplier. I imagine the vendor was happy to see us go.

Anyone know a Website designer who is creative and doesn't mind working with a committee? Cookies and ice cream are optional.

How To Increase Your Advertising Effectiveness

Do you advertise? Are you happy with the results? If not, you're not alone. Cost effective advertising is a challenge facing every business, regardless of size. Companies from the corner dry cleaner to General Motors look at the money they've spent to shove their message in front of the buying public and wonder "where did all that money go?" Too often the money would have done more good had it been left in the cash drawer.

Advertising is a very effective method of increasing business. Without it, you grow only by word of mouth, which is extremely limiting. Used right, it can take you into new territories, introduce new products, and expand into additional industries. Doing business without advertising is like making faces in the dark. You know what you're doing, but no one else does.

To make your advertising pay off, here are 10 ½ ways to increase effectiveness:

1. **Use the right media** – use media that match the demographics of your target client base. Every advertising salesperson knocking at your door knows their audience. Pick who will reach your

target audience. You don't have to do any fancy studies. If their listeners are under 25 and your customers have gray hair, use someone else.

2. **The message is key** – focus on benefits. Why are you better than the firm down the street? Create an advertising theme around your differences and give the prospect specific reasons to come to you.

3. **Repetition, repetition** – Remember how often your 3 year old wanted to hear the same book? Your prospect audience is the same way. There is no such thing as too often. But too seldom can be disastrous. Use your budget in ways that give frequent play. In print, consider several smaller ads in the same issue. A very unscientific rule of thumb is to have your relatives read the newspaper you are in. If they don't see your ads without searching, you're not in large enough or often enough.

4. **Be creative** – Lead, don't follow. Restrain the temptation to hold a Midnight Madness Sale like everyone else. Do something unique that stands out from your competition. This is an opportunity to create a personality for your business – use it. Hint: try cross industry concepts, like a dry cleaner having a tent sale.

5. **Teamwork wins** – Use the advertising sales team– they have experience in what works. Keep them focused on results. As the ads run, meet with them to review responses and discuss mid course corrections.

6. **Be respectful** – treat your customers with respect. Capture the attitude of inviting friends over for dinner. While blaring ads work for some companies, you'll likely find more success

considering potential clients as friends you haven't met yet rather than people who should be spending money in your shop.

7. **Lead them to action** – what do you want them to do as a result of your ad? Make the action you expect readers to take crystal clear. If you want them to call, print the phone number in large bold type. If you want them to visit, give a map. Consider reply coupons and web responses too.

8. **Be prepared** – before you place your ad, check your response system. Are you ready for inquiries? If prospects call, who do they get? If voice mail is their first hurdle, you're going to lose a large number who simply won't put up with your phone tree. Then you'll consider your advertising campaign a failure when it was your phone system that had the holes in it.

9. **Keep track** – Log all calls and follow each to a sale. The only way to truly know if your advertising is cost effective is to track results. If you don't take in more than the ads cost, it wasn't worth it.

10. **Selling is your job** – remember that the most advertising can do is get prospects to inquire. The job of selling is yours. The sale is yours to make or not. Make it. If someone is interested enough to call, you're half way to a sale. Now take it the rest of the way with your sales team.

10.5 **Have fun** – Let your wild inner self loose a bit. This is a place where being funny, being goofy, even being weird can pay off. Advertising is a great deal of fun – enjoy it.

Good advertising can increase your client base dramatically. You can tell thousands of people how great

your business is and why they should come to you. Used
wisely, advertising can dramatically ramp up the growth
patterns of a business.   Use these techniques to increase
advertising effectiveness and make the whole process
enjoyable and successful.

How to Hire Effective Sales People

Are you frustrated trying to recruit and hire the right sales people for your business? If so, you're not alone. Hiring, training, motivating, and compensating sales people is one of the most frustrating and difficult challenges facing virtually every firm from McDonalds to IBM.

Selling is a skill. Most people do not do it well. Because good selling skills are relatively rare, having proficient sales men and women represent your company to potential customers gives you a significant edge over the competition.

Selling is persuading a prospect to buy from you. The salesman's job begins when the customer says NO! Selling is not simply presenting your product and babbling on with a rehearsed litany of features. It is identifying the customers needs, making a presentation that serves those needs, overcoming objections, and closing effectively. Having people who know how to do this well on your staff is crucial to your growth.

The challenge of hiring a good sales force is usually one of finding people with both sales ability AND the required technical knowledge for your business. The decision frequently comes down to whether to pick people with technical knowledge and train them to be sales people or to hire people with sales skills and teach them the technical information.

My experience is that you are generally better off hiring sales people and either teaching them the technical stuff or partnering them with someone from the technical department. Too often technically proficient sales reps get so bogged down in the mechanical aspects of the product that they never get around to selling. They end up educating the customer and then losing the job to someone who knows how to sell.

The most important element of finding a good sales person is to have a clearly articulated sales program before you begin to recruit. Begin this process by making a complete outline of your sales position. This should include all of the following:

- **Specific Sales Goals** - What do you want this person or people to achieve? Increase sales by 10%? Add 3 new major clients? Recover lost clients? Identify several specific goals that you want the new salesperson to achieve.

- **Work Program** - What work performance do you expect? Call on 10 new prospects a week? Design flyers or newsletters to mail out? Cold call to telephone lists? Will they do their own letters, proposals, contracts and thus need to be proficient at word processing, spreadsheets, or contact management software.

- **Personal Attributes** - What personal attributes will contribute to success? Does the person need to be a self-starter, work with a team, have an eagerness to learn, be a good listener, be creative? Think about current sales people who are successful and consider which of their attributes you want repeated in new hires.

- **Compensation** - How are you going to motivate them through compensation? This is a science in itself. Write out the major elements of a clearly defined compensation package.

Once this is done, create an applicant package. This should be attractive and include a description of the company, your products, your clients, and your corporate goals. Tell a bit about the history, the current principals, and where you think the company will be in 5 years. Explain in detail the specific sales position you want to fill. Include most of the information from your comprehensive outline or include the actual outline so that an applicant reading it will understand exactly what is required of them and what working with you will be like.

Keep in mind you are selling the right person on joining your company. Good sales people have a lot of job opportunities -- you want them to come to work with you. Highlight the accomplishment aspects of the position. Explain the support staff they will have and be very clear about your sales goals. Finally, explain the compensation package and show how the salary and bonus program will look as an annual compensation package if sales goals are met. You will find this system very effective both in recruiting good people and also in helping people who are not appropriate eliminate themselves from consideration which saves you a bunch of interview time.

Once that is complete, consider where to find people with the industry knowledge and sales skills you need. One obvious source is your competitors. If someone working for a competitor is doing a good job selling against you, find a third party to see if they are interested in considering a change. This of course has several advantages: they bring new customers which are taken away from the competition and you reduce the effectiveness of your competition by taking away their good sales people.

Another excellent source is your clients. They are proficient in the industry and have many ideas of ways salespeople should represent your products. These insiders can also bring industry contacts and they could be up and running with minimal training. Call your customers and tell them you are looking for sales people. Ask them if they know anyone who is looking. If they happen to be going through a downsizing, they will jump at the chance to offer their employees possibilities when giving out pink slips.

Finally use plain old Help Wanted ads in industry trade publications as well as normal newspaper channels. Make your ads cheerful and attractive. Make your opportunity enticing so capable people will call.

When people contact you, send them the applicant package before you interview them. This gives them the opportunity to decide if the position is right for them. In the interview have them demonstrate an ability to sell. If you do not have the knowledge to evaluate selling skills, hire someone who can.

This is vital! You must determine how well someone can sell before you consider hiring them. Once they have proved their sales skills and you are satisfied with them in an interview, send them to accompany one of your current sales people on a sales call. Afterwards, debrief the applicant on how they would have done things differently. Make your selection of the best person based on the criteria in your initial outline of skill attributes combined with your own sense of who will fit in best to your company.

This is a lengthy process. Most people cut corners and don't implement all of it. The penalty for not hiring the right sales people is dramatic and very painful. You waste time and energy training someone who does not work out. You lose customer opportunities from inept handling of sales calls. And finally, when they don't work out, you have to start all over again.

Do it right the first time -- it's much easier.

Need Help?
Look in the Appendix for a Sample Sales Person Attributes form.

Managing Your Sales Force

Do you manage your sales force? Or since they are on commission do you assume they are doing the best they can and sit back to wait for the revenues they generate?

If you're taking the sitting back approach, you're losing a great deal of business as well as living with a higher than needed turnover in your sales force. Sales people need constant nurturing. They also need training, incentives, pats on the back, motivation, encouragement, discipline, goals, and leadership. Truly effective sales teams are the result of a strong leader. Once you have hired and fielded a team of capable sales people, your ongoing management of them will be the key to how successful they are.

Here are the six main components of managing an effective sales force:

Important Component I - Goals

If you don't know where you're going, it's a cinch that your sales force doesn't have a clue how to get you there. One of the most important elements of a successful sales program is clearly articulated goals that everyone agrees are realistic and attainable.

You need to articulate clear sales goals for each of the following:

- Sales to current clients

- Sales to new clients

- Referral business

Create these at the beginning of each year and refer to them in every sales meeting until the New Year's Eve Party. Compare goals to results at each meeting.

Important Component II - Procedures

Do you have written procedures for your sales process? You should. The reason for this is simple; it shows sales people what to do in the sales cycle. These people are representing your company. You don't want them deciding how to do it in the prospect's office.

Your written procedures should include all of the following:

- Each specific step of your sales process (initial call, enter name in computer system, send our brochure, make sales presentation) including assigning the person responsible for each step.

- Written new client form to be completed at initial client contact. It asks for the information you need to sell to and follow-up with each client.

- Computerized system of contact management to be entered for each new prospect.

- Formalized sales presentation.

- Specific collateral materials (brochures, product slicks, Thank You notes, etc.) and the sequence in which they are to be sent out.

- Prewritten form letters set up to mail-merge from your contact management system.

- Specific procedures for generating and presenting proposals.

- Procedures for closing the sale.

- Written answers to all possible customer objections.

- How to enter new client orders into your company's production or delivery system.

- New client credit procedures.

- Post sale follow-up procedures.

- Methods of getting referrals from current clients.

These all must be as clear and defined as possible. These elements are generally present in each sales progression and should be spelled out beforehand.

Important Component III – Training

Once a new salesperson goes through the basic two-week training program, most managers consider the training needs fulfilled. They are not. Use ongoing training to ensure that your sales procedures are understood and followed. Your sales people represent your company; don't let them go out without complete confidence in what they are doing. Do role playing in your sales meetings. Rehearse methods of overcoming objections. Give product knowledge tests. Have sales people calculate prices for sample orders, answer delivery questions, and discuss various customers' needs. Describe a customer scenario and listen to what questions they would ask and which of your products or services they would recommend.

Important Component IV – Logs

Which sales person has the best close ratio? How many inquiry calls do you get a week? Which promotions drew the best responses? Which sales person took the most new client calls? Was it the one with the most capability of closing?

Knowing these facts will help you do a better job of managing your sales force and also help you increase sales effectiveness.

Keep accurate logs of the following:

- Each customer inquiry including when the call came in. Note the advertising and promotions that ran and track results with the incoming calls.

- Which sales person took each inquiry – track the prospect all the way to a sale or no sale.

- Every sales person's outgoing calls and letters.

- Every sales person's sales presentations.

- All resultant new customer orders.

Calculate ongoing totals. How many inquiries are turned into sales presentations? How many sales presentations result in orders? By consistently monitoring performance, you will spot trends that can be corrected. You may find that Joe only turns 20% of the calls he takes into presentations, where Sally converts 45%. Clearly, something is missing from the way Joe is dealing with the calls. Listen to Joe's conversations with prospects. Determine where he is falling down. Typically if someone is underachieving, it's because they are not following your procedures. Work with underachievers to get their performance up to snuff. It's usually easier to replace bad habits than to replace people.

Important Component V - Motivation

This is perhaps the most overlooked element of sales force management. Too often managers think that the commission from the sale is motivation enough for their sales person. It is not. Sales people are extremely emotional people. They need a great deal of emotional feedback. They need to know that management appreciates their successes. Provide them with support for their sales challenges. Don't let them feel like they are fighting the battle alone. Congratulate them for work well done. It will do wonders for the next sale.

Create motivation through contests, encouragement, and support. Have a contest for the most new orders this month. Give them additional incentive to perform. Publicly congratulate a salesperson every time they close a particularly difficult or large sale.

Important Component VI – Sales Meetings

Finally, hold at least weekly sales meetings. This is working with the sales force as a team. This is your huddle before the ball snap. This is your finger on the pulse of the new work coming into your company – don't treat it lightly.

Effective sales meetings include all the following:

- Written agendas

- Congratulations to individuals for sales successes

- Review of sales procedures and refresher training

- Comparison of actual sales results with projections and previous year's results

- Discussions of close ratios

- Discussions of specific clients sales people are trying to close

- Role playing of customer objections and how to overcome them.

- Discussions of any delivery of customer service problems.

- Discussions of coming marketing programs – make sure your sales people know what your ads offer, what promotions you are going to be running, etc.

- Discussions of issues and problems that are hampering the sales process

- Motivation to increase performance for the coming week

Sales people need a great deal of ongoing support. They feel that they are carrying the banner for the company and typically they feel under-appreciated and under-loved. They need constant reassurance they are doing a good job. Work with your sales force. Recognize and reward them. They will bring in more business and you'll all enjoy the process much more.

Need Help?
Look in the Appendix for a Sample Sales Person Log form.

Compensating Your Sales Force

How clear is your compensation agreement for your sales force?   Can you recite their commission structure from memory? Can each sales person?

Too often managers create a complex legal document for a commission agreement but the end result is making the attorney happy. It does nothing to motivate sales people because they don't understand it.   One quick test of your current compensation program is to have your sales people calculate their commission for a hypothetical sale. Compare their calculations to yours. If they can't do it from memory or there is any discrepancy between their calculations and yours, you have a problem.   More critically, your compensation agreement is not only a failure as a motivating tool, you are going to have arguments when paychecks are issued. That's the time when you should be celebrating, not fighting.

There are several steps to creating a compensation program that will effectively motivate your sales force and eliminate confusion. Here they are:

1. Put it in Writing – Is your sales force compensation agreement in writing? Is it current or have you amended it as you've gone along but haven't bothered to update the written agreement?   If you don't put it in writing and give a copy to each person, I guarantee you will have disagreements when it's time to pay the commissions. Write it down and keep it handy. Your compensation agreement is the ongoing motivational force you are using to improve sales performance. Your sales force should have it at the ready as a constant reference.

2. KISS (Keep It Simple Stupid) − If your sales people don't understand the agreement it won't motivate them. All elements of your compensation package must be so straightforward that any three people calculating a commission will come up with the exact same number. If your sales people are spending hours calculating commissions, that's time they're not out selling your products.

To keep it simple, don't try to accomplish every element of their work objectives through the compensation plan. Identify 3 or 4 elements that are key and base commissions on them. For example, don't attempt to motivate people to make phone calls, do follow-up and send out letters by paying them for each accomplishment. These do not bring in revenues to the company and as such should not be payment items. Compensate sales people for sales.

3. Make it Consistent − Do each of your sales people receive the same compensation for the same performance? This is critical to teamwork, and turnover. Sales people expect fairness. If you are not compensating them the same for identical performance you'd better have a reason they can understand and accept.

Of course, this does not mean that all sales people will receive the same salary. You may pay different people different base salaries based on experience and performance. And different sales successes will yield different individual paychecks. But overall, there had better be consistency in your compensation plans for people doing like jobs with like skills. If you are not doing this and believe that the differences are justified, create different job titles so you can match the varied compensation levels with truly different jobs.

4. Get Rid of the Limits – Do you have limits on how much your sales people can earn? If so, you have limits on how successful your company will be. Your corporate objective should be to hope your salespeople earn obscene amounts of money. If your compensation plan is structured so resentment will accrue from their success, something is wrong. Sales people bring in the sales that allow everyone else to have a job. Compensate them for their performance and structure their compensation so when they do well, everyone in the company is happy.

5. Include Goals and Expectations – Your commission plan is the implementation program for your corporate goals. Outline goals right in their package. Make it clear that these are the goals to be met. Then design compensation of commissions and bonuses for meeting and exceeding those goals.

Do you want them to call on new customers, answer phone inquiries, help design marketing strategies? Do you want them to increase business by 10%? Do you want 25 new customers, $10,000 in new sales, $150,000 in monthly gross revenues? Put it in the agreement even if it isn't part of their compensation package.

6. Form a Committee – Setting compensation is just the sort of dirty work that deserves a committee. Include outsiders, managers, the sales manager, and at least one sales person.

Did you just yell, "No Way!" Does having a salesperson decide their own commission sound like letting the fox design the lock for the hen house? Who better to understand the challenges facing the sales team? Who better to point out flaws in your program? Who better to create a plan that will actually motivate the sales team to sell more? Pick someone who is objective and articulate. Their contributions to the compensation committee will be invaluable.

Each sales person's compensation should consist of 3 elements: Base salary or draw; commission for sales made; and bonuses for goals met. The last is typically a group effort and likely will result in splitting money among the sales team. Shared bonuses are a good method of motivating sales people to help each other's customers even though they don't get a direct commission from the individual sale.

The right commission structure can make a huge difference in your revenues. Take the time to structure it correctly and then work with your sales force to make sure it is a motivating tool. You'll pocket the results.

Need Help?
Look in the Appendix for a Sample Sales Person Employment Agreement including compensation terms.

Survival Guide for the Holidays

I was having breakfast at McDonalds a while back when I overheard someone holding his sales meeting right there in a booth at the Golden Arches. He had gathered his staff over Egg McMuffins and although wearing a Halloween tie, was giving them advice on how to market during the Christmas season. I was so impressed with his merchandising philosophy that I eavesdropped a while and when he finished his sales meeting, I went over and introduced myself.

He is Doug Golden, area manager for Radio Shack stores. A few minutes of listening to him and it is obvious that Doug has helped more than one Santa deliver a gift or two down chimneys of past Christmases. Ten years in the front trenches of sales has taught Doug a few tricks about merchandising in the Ho Ho Ho season. He has a dogmatically practical view of the season and encourages his store managers to make the most of it with better techniques.

I asked him to share a few pointers with the rest of us. Here are his recommendations:

Just Looking – when a customer says they are "Just Looking," answer with, "That's fine." Then look

with them. Do not leave the customer, but stay with them
to assist with advice and consultation. When they find
something they like, be there at the ready.

Follow the HOT routine:
- Help the Customer find what they came in for
- Offer them a great deal
- Tell them why they are fortunate to be shopping
  with you -- great service, wide variety, all the ways
  you stand out from your competition

Take the List – Ask who else is on their list. You
have items they didn't know you carried. Discuss the
other people on their gift list and make gift suggestions for
each one.

Don't Sell Just the Item – If they purchase a
remote control car, sell them batteries, battery charger and
a warranty. Do this for two reasons. When a child
receives the gift on Christmas or Hanukkah, you and your
customer both want him or her to be able to whip it out
of the box and drive it around right away. More important
from the store's standpoint, profits are in the accessories.
Increased sales here show up quickly on the bottom line.

Spotlight Items – Customers get confused over
the myriad of product selections available to them. Pick
your favorite item in each category. Put it on sale.
Rehearse your sales staff on its features. When a customer
stands bleary eyed in front of a wall of 10 VCR's, help
them select one by leading them to the Spotlight Item.
Explain why it's the best and help them make the decision
to purchase it.

Packages – Customers are on overload during the
holiday season. Make things simpler for them and more
profitable for you by putting together product packages.
For example, offer an iPod package that includes the unit,
speakers, battery charger and warranty. Price the entire
group as one unit. Customers make one purchase decision

and leave with everything they need. You sell more and make more in the process.

Smile, smile, smile – No one wants to know you've been there 12 hours. Keep plugging with a happy smile on your face and a song in your heart. Greet every single customer with enthusiasm and energy. There will be plenty of time for rest during the doldrums of January.

Merchandise By Interest Group – Rather than put all the remote cars together, put all the items for teenage boys together. Then shoppers can select from among a group of products that fit the person they are shopping for.

Exit Surveys – These work much better in your store than they do in the polls. As people leave, ask them if they found everything they wanted. Many sales are lost from the simple fact that customers get tired of searching for their item from among the thousands on the shelves. Make sure if it's on your shelves and on their list, it's in their shopping bag when they leave.

Protect Your Assets – The holiday season is a busy one and a dangerous one. Crooks know you are going to be diverted from your normal vigilance as you rake in the bucks. Do the basics. Keep your back door locked. Keep the register locked. Keep the money safe and take it to the bank frequently.

The holiday season is an extraordinary season for merchants. For most companies, business is good no matter what you do. But with the right preparation and merchandising, business and your profits will be not just great, but extraordinary. Use them!

The Second Sale is the Hardest

You signed the client. You've worked for several months to complete their contract. You're finally ready to present your finished product. I don't care what your product, I don't care what your industry, I don't care who your client is, I'm going to tell you some things about how your customer is going to receive that product you've worked so hard to create for them:

- It won't match their expectations.

- It will be different from what they had pictured.

- If it's creative, they won't understand it.

- If it includes new ideas, they'll say, "We've never done it that way before."

- If it's bold, they will be afraid of it.

- If it's green, they wanted white.

Sound familiar? Unfortunately this is the standard process of delivering custom-made products to the client. You rush in full of excitement, the client sits there with skepticism. You rip the cover off and yell, "Eureka!" They start pointing out its faults.

You work very hard to sign the client in the first place. Then you invest the effort and creativity to create the product they are paying you for. Then on the day of delivery, instead of trumpets heralding your accomplishments, your presentation is to frowns on the faces of the very people you worked so hard to please. Visions of that last payment on the contract start floating out the window. What went wrong?

There are several reasons for glum faces at the time of delivery. The most common reason is: you didn't sell your delivery. You invested all that selling energy into making the first sale, selling the customer. But the *Second Sale*, selling them on the product you have created for them, is even more important. Just because the client choose to hire you, does not mean they completely accept what you create for them. You have to sell them all over again at the presentation of the product.

Here are some ways to make that presentation a little more successful:

Control your Audience – Make sure the principals will be at the presentation so you can explain the features directly to them. You don't want others to answer their questions after you leave. Get the principals to the presentation and answer their concerns yourself.

Enthusiasm is Contagious – Arrive full of excitement. Make it very clear that you have worked hard to create their product and you are very proud of it. Hint at how excited they will be when they see it.

Foreplay is Important – Don't rush in, unwrap the product, and yell, "Here it is!" You expect the product to speak for itself. It won't. Have a clearly planned delivery sequence and follow it. If your product is a physical item, cover it up and create a sense of suspense waiting for the unveiling.

Map Please – Go over their goals that the product was supposed to meet and make sure everyone is in agreement with them. These are, of course, what you discussed months ago at the initial project meeting. Now, reiterate them for the entire group. Remind your audience about where they want to go or they won't know if they got there.

Leave the Driving to Us! - Sell your finished product. Use terms like, "Wait till you see how we achieved this!" and "You'll love the way we created this other part!" Create a sense of expectation and excitement.

And Now a Drum Roll – With as much excitement and fanfare as you can muster, present the product. Taped music (including drum rolls) is a great enhancement. So are lights, banners, signs, and any other sensory elements. You want your client to be excited about your product. Do whatever you need to do to achieve that.

Watch This -- Demonstrate your product from start to finish. Make sure you continually refer back to the client's goals to remind them that your product does in fact meet their objectives. You just reminded everyone in the room of the goals list. By definition if your product meets those goals, it is acceptable.

Questions Please – Now ask for questions. Answer all of them referring to how the product met the goals. Keep bringing people back to that goal list – don't let them wander into new territory.

Isn't This Wonderful? – Before you leave, make sure the client agrees that you met their goals. Ask direct questions. Handle objections the same way you would in a sales call. Make sure everyone is comfortable with your product before you leave.

Delivering whatever you created for them is exciting for your company. It represents culmination of a long work effort. Most important it marks the time to get the final payment from the client. Put the same effort and enthusiasm into the *Second Sale* that you did selling them on retaining you. You and your client will both be much happier as a result.

Take Two and Call Me in the Morning

You're going to laugh when I tell this story, but I swear every word is true except for the name which I changed to protect the semi-innocent. A man I'll call Uncle George retired from the post office and started pursuing his life-long hobby of cooking. He wasn't satisfied with the spices that were available over the counter so he experimented with various combinations of his own until he invented what he thought was the perfect spice. His friends tried it, fell in love, and told him it would outsell "Old Bay."

Encouraged, he pillaged his savings account, paid to have a bottle and label designed, and had 50 cases of the stuff manufactured and shipped to his house. Uncle George's Fancy Spice had a snappy yellow and red label and looked great. You'd grab it off the shelf the next time you wandered the supermarket aisles for sure. Uncle George had the cases piled high in his garage and was ready to sell his way to national fame.

Since he knew anyone who tried Uncle George's Fancy Spice would love it, his sales tactic was the famous puppy dog close. Give out samples, let them find out for themselves how great it is, and fill the orders when they

poured in.   He drove around leaving samples at every
store and distributor he came to.   He gave samples to
relatives, his barber, his wife's boss, the car wash guys, the
video store clerk.   He knew his spice was extraordinary.
The phone would soon be ringing off the hook.

A year later Uncle George consulted me to help
determine why the success he thought was guaranteed had
so far eluded him.   He had spent the entire year
attempting to create a market for Uncle George's Fancy
Spice. But the phone never rang.   Cases of the stuff still
filled his garage.

As I listened to a deflated Uncle George tell his
tale of spice scorned, I idly played with the jar of Uncle
George's Fancy Spice he had brought me as a sample. As
I twirled it around between my fingers, I noticed
something pretty critical.

"There's no phone number on the bottle," I
stated, as soon as he gave me a chance to get a word in
edgewise.

"What do you mean?" was his quick response.

"How were people going to call you to order
more?"

A light dawned, slowly and grimly.   Uncle George
had driven 33,000 miles attempting to implement a
marketing plan with a serious fatal flaw.

We'll never know how many people would have
ordered Uncle George's Fancy Spice by the case if the
could have contacted him.   Perhaps he would have passed
Old Bay by now.

While you're chuckling over Uncle George's story,
I'll wager that your things are labeled so well either.   Put
this down and go examine everything of yours that ends
up in the customer's hands.   Look at your products, your
invoices,   your   faxes,   your   packaging,   and   your
documentation.   I'll buy lunch for anyone who has every
single item well marked.

Believe it or not, this incredibly important element is one of the most overlooked aspects of getting more business from customers. I recently talked to a software company that was trying to get rich by giving people a free sample of their software over the internet. They planned to sell additional products once users learned how good their software was. They had the same grim look on their face as Uncle George did when I asked if their phone number was imbedded into their free software. The tragedy here is that they are much more sophisticated with much more at stake.

If you concede that things could be improved in the phone number department, you can buy me lunch. And then use this checklist to make sure you are getting as much bang as possible from everything that arrives in your client's hands:

- Packing materials – is your packaging as clearly marked as it could be? Especially check anything that the customer will keep.

- Invoices – is your address and PHONE NUMBER on the invoice? You'd be surprised how many companies don't include phone numbers.

- Letterhead and fax sheets – think this is silly? How many times have you received a fax where the cutesy address and phone number at the bottom of the stationery has been cut off or rendered unreadable by the fax? Fax your letterhead to yourself and make sure everything is legible.

- Your products themselves. Is your phone number readily available on the product itself? Too often companies assume that having their phone number on the instructions is enough. Where are the instructions for the gas grill you bought 5 years ago?

- Your services — At our house we have a furnace and a hot tub (we have other stuff too, but these are the items that need service most regularly). The furnace people put a huge sticker with their phone number right on the side of the furnace. We always call them because we can find their phone number when we need it. The people who sold us the spa gave us a business card roughly a thousand years ago. When we need service, we call the first vendor in the phone book — we have no idea where that business card got lost. Putting your information on the client's products does two things. It gives the clients an immediate way to call you — and it conveys the impression that they can't call anyone else.

- Other stuff. I once worked with a newspaper who wanted to make sure their subscribers got the paper every day. I asked them where a customer would find the phone number to call on a day when their paper was missing.   "It's in the paper," they answered, slowly realizing it would do no good for someone who did not get a paper. We designed refrigerator magnets to give customers instant access to their phone number when needed.

- Instruction materials and manuals. I have a computer program that emphasizes friendly technical support all through their manual. They were so busy emphasizing it, they forgot to put their phone number in the manual. I had to call information to find out how to reach them. Sometimes the obvious is the place that eludes you.

Current customers are an excellent source of referrals and repeat business. However two things must happen before they refer or repeat. First they have to be satisfied with your products and services. Second they have to be able to reach you. Do the job right to ensure the first. Put your phone number on everything in sight to ensure the second.

Clean up your language

I was at the car wash the other day for my weekly auto bath. As I was standing peering through that huge window mesmerized by the torrent of water and suds and waiting for my familiar hood ornament to pop through the machinery, the owner of the car wash walked by. Upon seeing me, he smiled and commented, "You're here more often than I am."

I assume he was trying to say, "I'm glad you patronize our establishment so often," but it came across as "You come here too often." Not the message he wants to give to regular customers.

I was discussing this episode with a colleague a few days later and he launched into his own story of inept sales conversation. He had called a magazine to place an order for advertising. He had already made up his mind to place his ads with that periodical and was simply gathering information in preparation to placing his order. The first person he talked to, Helen, said, "You need to talk to Cynthia. She's the person in charge of that. I'm not really familiar with it." She then proceeded to give information regarding ad placement in spite of her earlier claim that she wasn't the right person.

A few minutes later, the aforementioned Cynthia called to say the information Helen had given was incorrect. She then said, "You have to talk to me in the future when you want to advertise." She proceeded to give instructions for placing ads and peppered every sentence with "You need to...."

My colleague built up a head of steam telling the story. "Let me tell you something, " he yelled waving a finger in my face even though I hadn't told him he needed to do anything. "I'm the client. I don't need to do anything -- including buy from them, which I didn't. I had made up my mind that they were the best publication for my advertising. But I got so mad at this girl telling me what I had to do, I refused to do business with them."

Here are two excellent examples of snatching defeat out of the jaws of victory. In both cases the sale was essentially made and then lost as the direct result of poorly chosen words. I don't go to the car wash as often, my colleague placed his advertising elsewhere.

If we were to go talk to the individuals whose careless words had hurt sales, they would not even remember the remarks they made, say nothing of understand how their careless choice of words hurt sales. The car wash owner thought he was welcoming me to his business. In Cynthia's case, I imagine she was proud she had given her customer such detailed information about what he "needed to do" to place his ad. And he did in fact "need to do" all she told him. He just resented the way she told him.

At the final juncture of a sale, the emotion of the moment is critical. Poorly chosen words can derail a successful sales presentation faster than a log on the train track. Yet many people fail to consider the words they use and fall into habits that ultimately hurt sales. More critical, people who do not consider themselves in a sales environment think their actions or words do not matter. They do! Everyone in the company who talks to a customer is part of your sales team, whether they know it or not. From the receptionist to the delivery person, each person can make or break a sale. Each person should be schooled on how to communicate with customers.

Mark Twain wrote, "If you wonder about the difference one word makes, consider the difference between Lightning and a Lightning Bug." The exact word is critical. Not using words that can create the wrong impression is just as vital. Words like "Buy" or "Sell" are traditionally a no-no. No successful auto salesperson would ever say to a customer, "Would you like to buy the red station wagon?" A family who had planned to have the red station wagon parked in their driveway that evening will still rebel against the word "Buy."

There are many ways to improve customer communications in your company. Here are the steps to do so:

1. Make a list of the forbidden words for your industry and your company. These should include all normal bad words and also specific words appropriate to your selling environment.

2. Write out scripts of how to handle questions so they are answered professionally whoever answers.

Change how you phrase commands to make it sound like you are a consultant, not an order giver. As Cynthia found, no one wants to be told "they need to" anything.

3. Be positive in your phrasing. Rather than tell the customer they can't take the car for a test drive over the weekend, suggest they take it Monday.

4. If possible, tape record your conversations with clients. There's nothing illegal about laying a tape recorder on your desk and recording your side of a phone conversation. You will be surprised at the way you come across. This is an extremely effective tool in improving your interaction skills.

5. Rehearse.   The only way to improve is to practice. Rehearse with a tape recorder. You may feel a bit silly standing alone in an empty room waving your arms around and giving your pitch. But that is not nearly as silly as you will feel when you watch a sale go down the drain from careless remarks.

Inept comments hurt sales.   In the examples above, they hurt directly and immediately. By following the steps listed, you can eliminate conversational missteps and make all your comments lead to the sale.

I have to go now – I'm getting the car washed. I just hope the owner doesn't see me sneak in.

Why did you leave me?

The mail at our house recently included a postcard from the local Lexus dealer reminding us to have our car serviced. It was one of those cutesy things that was personalized with our first names and included personal information like the model of our car. It told us what service we needed for our Lexus. It would have been a convincing example of how the car dealership truly cared about us as individuals except for one small fact. We sold the Lexus two years ago. They didn't even know we weren't customers any more.

Customers have a very effective way of telling you that they are unhappy with your products or services. They go somewhere else. When a customer stops doing business with you, do you know they've left? If you don't even know they've left, you have some pretty difficult marketing challenges ahead of you.

You need to know when a customer leaves you and you need to know why. And if you get word before they actually leave, do everything possible to keep them from leaving. You can't afford to constantly bring in new customers to replace ones that have gone away. It's much cheaper to keep the ones you have.

Admittedly the "Knowing when they leave," part can be tough. For most service providers, it's easy to tell when a customer wants a divorce. They have to call to cancel. You always know who your customers are. Retail businesses, however, typically don't know their customers. It's a bit more difficult to keep track of which customers are still on board, but it is no less important. In all cases put systems in place to alert you to defecting customers. Institute an interview process to determine why they are leaving. In the case of our sold Lexus, we had taken the car into the dealer for the inspection before selling it. They knew, or at least had the opportunity to know, that we were selling the car, but did nothing about it.

Departing customers are invaluable in several ways:

1. They alert you to problems. Customers leave for many reasons – they move, they change jobs, their kids go off to college, they change hobbies. You want to know one thing: Did they leave because of their issues or yours? There is little you can do about someone moving out of your area, but if their issues were from the way you do business, this is a signal of adjustments that need to be made. Departing customers are not alone in their opinions. Making changes now can prevent further erosion of your customer base.

They alert you to competitor offerings. If customers are defecting because of perceived benefits from competitors, you want to know about it immediately so you can take preventive action. You may want to offer similar promotions or pricing or you may need to educate your customers to the value of your services compared to their perceived value of the competitor's.

2. A significant percentage of lost customers can be recovered by taking the time to communicate with them. Identify their issues and work with them to correct those problems as quickly as possible.

Until your former customer becomes comfortable with another vendor there is a window in which you can win them back. A recent survey we did for a newspaper found that 5% of their lost customers would have stayed if someone had solved their problems. That is about the least expensive method of gaining an increase in business possible – a telephone call.

Customers are remarkably quiet when it comes to telling you about problems. They typically "Vote with their feet" by going to a competitor rather than tell you what you can do to keep them. You have to take the initiative to communicate with them.

Here are some ways to prevent lost customers and to recover a few of those who do leave:

- Interview your customers. You do not know how well you are doing in meeting their needs without constantly asking them.

- Station someone at the exit doors to ask every customer if they found everything they were looking for, especially those that leave without buying something. They came into your store with some purchase in mind. The fact that they are leaving empty handed signals they didn't get it. Learn why.

- Identify the moment when a customer leaves you. If you are in a business where the customer has to notify you to leave, attempt to keep them on board when the customer calls to cancel. If that is not possible, do exit interviews and tabulate the results. You should know what percentage of customers left for what reasons.

- Call or write to every customer who leaves you within two weeks of their departure. Ask them what you can do to get them back.

- Make sure all avenues of communication are open and easy for the customer to use.

Customers who leave obviously hurt business. You immediately lose the revenues from their purchases. And if they are part of a trend, additional revenues will be lost as others follow suit. Major business losses can be avoided by determining early on that something is changing. Make sure you keep all your customers. It's much cheaper than finding new ones. And don't send cutesy postcards unless you know someone still owns the car.

May I Help You?

I went into a record store the other day and was greeted by the ubiquitous, "May I Help You?" Was this salesperson actually asking my permission to wait on me?

This greeting is non-functional as a sales tool. It only results in a sale to someone who was already committed to buying. It does not convert a "just looking" into a sale. Yet most retailers, after spending thousands in advertising to get the prospect into the door, allow their sales people to fall into the "May I Help You?" trap rather than train them in better selling skills. If you are a retailer and your sales people are using "May I Help You?" as their opening line, you are losing 30% of the sales you could be making.

There are several reasons why this is a bad greeting. First it gives the sales person no place to go conversationally when the customer says "No." You're allowing the customer to dictate the relationship. Although you think of "May I Help You?" as a friendly greeting, the customer hears "May I SELL You?" Customers run away from being sold to.

Second, when the customer says "No," it's a negative beginning. Remember the old school of negotiating where the first thing to do is get both parties to agree on something? You want customers nodding their heads 'Yes' when they come into your store. Start on a positive. Even if you have to discuss the weather, open with something you can agree on. "It's a nasty day outside, isn't it?" has a great deal more conversational possibilities than "May I Help You?"

Finally, "May I Help You?" is not an exploratory question. If the customer says "Yes" you still have no idea why they came into your store. Typically if the sales person has not been trained any better than to say "May I Help You?" they likely have few other skills to identify the customer's needs. Without knowing the customer's needs, the sales clerk can't help them, they can only ring up the order once the customer has waited on themselves. Even the one word change to, "How may I help you?" starts to explore ways to meet the customer's needs.

You invest a great deal of money to bring customers into your store. You pay higher rent for a high traffic location. You pay advertising expenses to create name recognition. You pay for store signage and attractive entrance designs. All of this results in only one action by the prospective customer: walking through your door. After that, whether or not a sale occurs and how large that sale is, depends entirely on your sales force. Whether they actively sell to customers or just ring up the cash register will determine how effective all the other marketing expenses were.

Here's how to maximize your sales opportunities once a potential customer walks through the door:

Start with a friendly introductory greeting to your store. "Good morning, welcome to Big Sounds Records and Tapes," is an excellent start. Next, start building a relationship with the customer by introducing yourself. "I'm Leon Frank, what can I show you today?" Personally I like to learn the customer's name up front and I'll ask for it if the customer doesn't offer it as part of a greeting.

Learning the customer's name seems contrary to most retailer sales people because they believe that there is an unwritten rule you can't get to know your customer in retail. No one wrote such a rule.

Once you have introduced yourself and gotten the customer's name, start working with them to identify and solve their needs. Use open-ended questions designed to start a conversation and learn more about them. "Tom, who's your favorite artist?" is a good start. Here are some other opening lines:

- Are you here looking for something for yourself or a friend today?

- Our CD's make great gifts to have on hand.

- Have you seen the new DVD players?

- What's your favorite type of music?

- Are you interested in the latest technology?

- Which kind of music do you like: easy listening or jazz?

Holiday seasons offer even more possibilities: "Who on your gift list do you still have to buy for?" is an excellent discussion topic.

Continue to engage the customer in conversation by tying in elements of your business. Introduce interesting information that will add to the customer's enjoyment of your products. For example, if the customer tells you they like Easy Listening Music, you might respond with, "Neil Diamond just introduced a new album. Would you like to hear it?" Do all you can to act more like a consultant than a sales person. You are now working with them to help make good purchase decisions, rather than sell to them.

Questions that explore their needs are not considered selling by the customer. They are interactive, considerate, and truly help them achieve their goals.

Consultative selling is extremely effective and customers go away having purchased more than they would have and enjoying the process far more.

When customers come into your store, "Help Them Buy." But don't ask for permission to do so.

Need Help?
Look in the Appendix for 21 ways to Prevent May I Help You?

How to Charge for Consulting Services

Do you sell complex products? If you do, and perhaps even if you don't, you've undoubtedly provided a great deal of free consulting help to clients who do not have the technical sophistication to place their order correctly. You have other clients who do not need the technical hand holding so there is a large disparity in the amount of free service provided to each client. One type of customer consumes nearly an hour each time they order because they need so much explanation, the other takes 10 minutes. It is very difficult to charge for the additional expertise you must provide to get the order right, even though by giving it, you truly are offering different value for the same price.

It seems like a "No Win" situation. If you don't provide less educated customers with the advice they need, they order the wrong things and expect you to redo the order when it does not meet their needs. If you attempt to tack on a consulting fee to their invoice they holler just the same.

Here is a system that works pretty well at solving this problem by bringing in additional revenues for the consulting they need at the same time, eliminating the warranty issues of the unsophisticated client ordering the wrong items.

Offer two different levels of pricing and warranties. Let the client identify their level of sophistication and expertise before placing their order. They choose a different warranty along with a different pricing system.

For clients with the expertise to correctly place an order without handholding, give a lower price and no promise that it will work for them. Simply guarantee that the product shipped will be exactly what they ordered. You do not guarantee that it will work in their application. They take full responsibility for the correct configuration and if they are wrong, they pay to have the order redone.

For clients who want more help, give more personal service and a more comprehensive guarantee. Of course this goes with a higher price. Add a charge onto the invoice for consulting services, then go ahead and consult with them about their needs and application. You configure the order to their application. And guarantee your product will work in their application. You are the one responsible for making sure their order meets their needs. If it doesn't, you pay to have the order redone.

By giving the client the choice of two different guarantees along with two different price structures, most of the resistance for paying for consulting services will evaporate. You will spend less time taking client orders. You will receive revenues for the time you do spend providing customers with the expertise they need. And you'll reduce your exposure guaranteeing products to customers who ordered the wrong product without consulting with you.

Customers will get what they need. Since you are providing consulting services to establish their needs (and getting paid for it), you can take the extra time to work with them and to educate them. The end result will be better, more sophisticated customers with a lower percentage of redo work for your company. You and your customers will be much happier all the way around.

How to Increase Revenues through Service Agreements

Does your business provide services to clients on an "as needed" basis? As a result, is your income all over the board from month to month? One month you have plenty of income, the next month you're struggling. To improve the stability of your cash flow as well as increase total service revenues, consider establishing Service Agreements with your clients. Under a Service Agreement, clients pay a fixed monthly fee regardless of the amount of service you provide them.

This immediately does several things for you. It gives you predictable income – your service revenues are the same every month. It increases your total service revenues, since you are now the only vendor your clients will turn to. You save on paperwork -- you don't need to invoice each service call. You can provide services more immediately, you don't need to wait for the client to generate Purchase Orders.

For your clients, it offers a stabilized cash flow – they know their monthly service expenses. It reduces their expenses in the same ways, no Purchase Orders or invoices. Service will be provided more quickly since they simply pick up the phone and call.

Setting up a Service Agreement program takes a bit of homework. Among other things, you need to establish how much to charge each client. You don't want to set it too high, or they won't buy. Too low, and you take it in the shorts by providing more services for less revenues.

To establish how much to charge, do a comprehensive analysis of each clients' service history. For each client it is vital to know whether you are their only vendor. If they have been using other vendors, their invoice history with your company does not represent their entire service needs. Good news here - a Service Agreement with you will capture all their business and beat out your competition for their business.

Calculate the average service bills per month per client. Then calculate monthly averages by types of equipment serviced and also other identifiable parameters that are relevant to your industry. Determine how predictable maintenance costs are. At the end of this process, you should have the following:

- Monthly average service expense for each client

- Monthly average service expense for each piece of equipment you service

- Monthly average service expense for each service you provide

- Additional averages as appropriate

Now, using the averages, decide whether to set your pricing based on equipment, by client, or by some other determining factor.

Once you have done all this homework, start writing the terms of the Service Agreement program. Spell out every element clearly so clients have no doubt what they are getting. Generally you will offer each client a fixed monthly for whatever service they require. If their service needs are so unpredictable you can't risk a fixed price, limit the number of hours you'll provide under the agreement.

Once you have a written program, SELL it to your clients. Prepare a package for each individual client that includes the Service Agreement, the benefits to them, and a comparison to their past service costs. By demonstrating how it will save them money as well as give them predictable monthly expenses they should be pretty receptive to the concept.

For client companies who decide not to go with the program right away, continue to remind them of the option at periodic intervals. Every six months or so include a brief note with their monthly invoice reminding them of the Service Agreement Program. And at least once a year, visit them in person to bring up the program again.

Finally, be sure to monitor your Service Agreement Program closely. Even though you no longer need to invoice clients for each service call, keep meticulous records and conduct an annual audit of each client's needs compared with their payments. You'll likely need to adjust each year to make sure you are in balance.

The Service Agreement Program works for many businesses. Create it, design it, and then sell it. Once you have invested the time and effort to set up the program, you will see service revenues increase along with a reduction of your administrative costs.

Need Help?
Look in the Appendix for a Sample Service Agreement.

A Customer in the Store is Worth 15 in the Trees

Last year I had a custom computer made by a local company I'll call Frog Computers. I called Frog the other day to discuss upgrades to my machine. My used-to-be state of the art machine now bogged down with the new state of the art software. The tech support person thought its sluggish performance might be memory rather than a slow CPU. He could, he promised, diagnose the problem and add memory or upgrade the processor, whichever I chose. More important, they could do it quickly.

I unplugged the maze of life support cords from the back of the computer and hauled the machine into Frog's hospital. Shortly, the tech support guy informed me that my beleaguered computer was indeed slower than it should be. However, they did not have any memory in stock (not mentioned when I called) and the only person in the whole store who could give me a quote on a CPU upgrade was out and would not return today (also not mentioned during my call). Aforementioned person would call me tomorrow with the information I needed. Disappointed, I hauled the computer back to my office, reconnected all the plugs and cables, and waited for Frog's only person in the store expert to call. He never did.

It was time to find a company whose only person in the store who knew the answers was actually in the store. I had already invested a couple hours and my trusty machine still got indigestion when processing graphics. I headed off to a competitor who could give me immediate solutions.

The scary message in this example is this. Frog Computers spends a great deal of money advertising to bring in new customers. Yet when they had me, a prospective customer standing in their store with checkbook in hand, they failed to make the sale. In fact, they lost both the sale and the customer. Now they have to bring in a new customer to replace me before any other newcomers translate into growth.

This is the other side of the "advertising for growth" sword. If you lose customers along the way, you have to bring in replacements before additional customers are translated into growth. If your advertising brings in 12% new customers and you lose 8%, you have a growth of 4%. Keep your current customers and growth shoots up to 12%.

Too often businesses are so intent on bringing in new business that they overlook the additional revenues available from their current customers. Or worse they lose both revenues and customers while they focus on new prospects. Does this happen in your business? If so, here is a marketing concept that will immediately increase revenues and cost you exactly nothing to implement. Sell more to your current customers.

Here are some ways to increase sales to current customers, many of whom aren't necessarily standing in your store.

- Whenever you hear from a current customer for any reason, a question, an inquiry about new products, a request for help, even with a complaint, make sure you listen and solve their problems -- completely. Don't give them the smallest reason to look to other vendors for solutions. Your competition will know exactly how to capitalize on that opportunity. Get your customers in the habit of depending on you. Complete a form every time a customer contacts you. List what the customer needed and how it was provided to them. Have your sales department review the completed forms every day. They can follow up on sales opportunities as well as ensure that all customers' needs are met. My guess is Frog's sales department didn't even know I was there itching to spend money with them.

- Anticipate your customer's needs. You know exactly what product your customer has. You know when they bought it. You should know how they use it. Contact them when it is time for service or when an update might help them. Keep them informed and remind them they are your customer. Don't wait for your customers to call you –call them.

- Kill them with communication. Send newsletters. Send information on the latest products. Tell about special sales. Send flowers. Send Arbor Day cards. Make your customers feel like they have a relationship with you.

- Do you know your customers? Every time I went into Frog Computers, they had different employees. No one recognized me or for that matter, my computer. Find ways to identify your customers so you can make them feel special. Give them special ID. Identify them in your computer system. Let them know how important your relationship is to them every time they come in or call.

Current customers represent a great deal of potential business. You know how to reach them. You know their buying habits. You know the products they bought from you. You don't have to spend one cent to go out and find them – they're right there in your database. Show them that they are part of your family and that you are their only source for additional purchases. They're already inclined to shop with you -- make it easy for them to continue to do so.

Then when you do bring in new customers, those revenues translate immediately to growth for your company.

Web Mania

In less than 3 years *AMAZON.COM* grew from an idea to a company worth over $2 Billion with no store, no catalog, no telephone, and no inventory. They accomplished every bit of that growth using a single web site.

What have you done with your web site?

Virtually every company, from General Motors to the corner dry cleaner has their own web site. But most people who anguished over every word to develop a web site last year, typically haven't done a thing with it after calling all their friends and relatives to see it.

The web is changing rapidly. Many of the truisms of 6 months ago are no longer operative. A year ago, there was virtually no "walk in traffic" to a web site. You had to steer prospects to your site yourself. Now there can be new traffic to your site from people "surfing" the web. Search engines can bring in new shoppers by the droves. However, to take advantage of the power of a web site, you must design and market it correctly.

Your web site should be an active part of your marketing program. It should be bringing new business into your company. If it's not, get busy and make your site work for you. Here's how:

- Establish clear goals of the site. Who is your on-line target? Is that different from the off-line customer? What is on your site that makes visitor want to bookmark and revisit?

- All off-line advertising should include the web address. Include it on business cards, letterhead and brochures. More important, make sure everyone in the company, from the receptionist to the CEO knows your web site address.

- Register the site with all the major search engines. Then reregister - it's an on going process.

- Have your site listed on all industry specific directories you can find for your industry. Most are free or have minimal fees.

- Consider advertising on other web sites to direct customers to your site.

- Update your site often - outdated material is a telltale sign that you don't take it seriously. (Don't you just hate to see Christmas decorations still up on Valentines day?)

- Maintain your Site - If you are not creating it yourself, consider having the site designed with a back-end "administrative program" which allows you to edit existing elements or add new information without help from the web gurus. Deciding on this at the beginning can save you a lot of heartache in the long run.

- Don't Assume Anything - Although there are more and more Internet users every day, the majority of people on-line are relative newcomers to the age of Technology.

- Unless your target audience is a specific industry that is going to fully understand how to utilize your web site, design it so it's easy enough for your grandmother to understand.

- Make An Impression - You have only 10 seconds to make an impression on your web site visitor, especially one who has found you as a result of surfing. That means that if your site is not visually appealing or does not have something of interest for the user, they will be moving on to the next one in a real hurry.

- Provide Useful Information - Content is king! Put yourself in your visitor's perspective. Your site should intrigue the user enough to keep them there and "push" them through it by tempting them with information that occurs by taking further action in your site. Throughout your site, keep in mind items that your user might find helpful; things that may not necessarily be about you or your business. For example, useful tips, lessons, links to other related or complementary sites, contests, how to get something free, etc. Be an industry resource.

- Be Interactive - One of the most exciting things about the Internet as a medium is that it allows users to interact with it, something that no other medium does. Create interactivity. Use click-on buttons, text links, optional selection features, fill-in forms and audio or video components. A web site that is only text is really no "fun" for the user, and will probably not be visited again.

- Make Responding Easy – include response devices that are easy to find and user friendly to use within your site. Make asking for more information or even ordering your products as convenient as a mouse click. People on the web want to use it as their communication system with you. Give them plenty of opportunity to contact you from your site.

- Promote, Promote, Promote -- Draft a press release to submit to both traditional and on-line media.   Do   a   small   direct   mail   campaign announcing your site to your clients or a list of prospects. Consider hiring a web site marketing consultant or firm who will tailor a campaign – locally, nationally or globally -- for you and your target audience.

Web sites have grown in usefulness over time. If you aren't using your site as part of your overall marketing strategy, you are missing out on a very inexpensive method of reaching and selling customers. You can give them pages of full color text, graphics, and photos for an absolute fraction of the cost of any other method. Look at the websites of competitors and of companies that you like to do business with, then make your web site the best of the lot.

You may not grow to the size of Amazon.com, but you certainly can use a great deal of their ideas to make your website and then your company more successful.

How Successful is Your Advertising?

I had lunch with a business associate the other day. The discussion covered the usual topics: politics, clients, business ideas. We told lies and war stories over salads, talked about specific projects over the entrees. I asked her how well her advertising program was working. I was specifically interested in one print ad I had seen. I liked it and assumed it would draw a pretty good response.

To my surprise, she answered that she had been very disappointed in the ad's response. After running it for several months, she had not gotten a single new client out of it. I couldn't understand this. The ad had many elements of good advertising: it was in the right publication to reach her audience, it stood out from the surrounding ads, it was well designed, and quickly got the reader's attention. She ran it regularly enough so it should draw some pretty consistent response. So why wasn't it working?

We talked more about that ad and advertising in general. It soon became clear that the ad was in fact drawing quite well. She was getting 4 – 6 calls from it a week. But she hadn't signed one new client from the responses, so felt the ad wasn't working.

Was it the ad? Or was it her ability to make a sales presentation and close the sale?

Too often business managers picture a very simple formula for advertising.

Spending more for ads = more revenues.

If you own a McDonald's, you're probably right. Advertising is that simple. Customers see a catchy ad and go to the golden arches to buy stuff. No client education is required when they come through the door. Once their in the store, they buy. Your staff does not make a sales presentation. There is no deliberation on the part of the consumer. Customers don't come into McDonald's for an estimate and then go home and think it over.

However, for the 99% of the businesses who are not fast food franchises, advertising generates an inquiry, NOT A SALE. Prospects do think it over after they listen to your presentation. No one sees an ad for an advertising agency or a car or custom software and calls to purchase. The most action you can get a prospect to take from any advertisement, from snappy television spots to direct mail, is to make an inquiry.

Once the prospect calls, it's up to you to make the sale. As my associate found, this can be the most difficult aspect of marketing. Finding prospects who are interested is relatively easy. Converting that interest into a sale is not.

Inquiries as a result of seeing an ad are the most critical juncture in the process of selling. The slightest obstacle in the prospect's path at the time of inquiry can result in losing them. If your receptionist leaves them on hold for 5 minutes or your phone mail tree is impossible to wander through, that prospect is history. The competition will have a new client and you will never know they called you first. One day you will be sitting over lunch groaning that you just poured a bucket of money into advertising and the results wouldn't fund the salad bar special.

To prevent that groaning lunch, work through the entire response process before you place the ad. Who is going to answer the phone? Are they going to take the call or are they going to refer it to a sales person? If you have more than one sales associate, how are you going to allocate the calls? What information is the sales person going to obtain while on the phone with the prospect? Do you have a prospect information form ready to fill out when they call? Write a phone script including the answers to most common questions and rehearse every sales person. In retail, do all the same things. The only difference is, you're facing your prospect.

Make sure every one from the receptionist to the sales department is completely familiar with your ads. Print copies of the ads along with dates of publication and the publication they will run in. Give copies to the entire staff. Put them on the bulletin board. If the ads are on the radio or television, make sure copies are available to play. List all elements of what you're offering in your advertising and give a copy of the list to each staff member. If you are offering specific products, make sure staffers know where the item is. If you feature a lawnmower for a great price and your sales people don't know where that model is, you will conclude your advertising failed because you didn't make any sales. Finally, track every incoming call including the following:

- Date of call, inquiry, or customer visit

- Whether they are a prospect who matches your client demographics – you want to know if the ad is pulling the wrong people into your business

- Name, company, and phone number of prospect

- Which sales person took the inquiry

- What ad prospects had responded to

- What product or service they were interested in

This will help you do several critically important things. First it will track responses to specific ads. You can immediately tell which ads are pulling and which ones aren't. It will also track the effectiveness of every sales person. You might want to start allocating calls according to success ratios, rather than evenly distributing them across the sales force. If someone is selling to inquiries while others are not, reward that person and the company by giving him or her more calls.

Advertising is an effective way to bring in new prospective clients. But the relationship at the inquiry stage is tenuous at best. The slightest bump in the road can upset it. Make sure there are no obstacles on the path to sales success.

Whether you groan about the cost or boast about your success at your next lunch depends on how well you convert interest to sales. Your job is not finished when you place the ad, it's just started.

Making Trade Shows Pay Off

Do you exhibit at Trade Shows? Do you enjoy the experience? Do you generate enough new sales to justify the expense of exhibiting?

Trade shows can be a great way to find new customers. They can also be a great way to spend a lot of money with little return. Unless you design and implement a specific trade show marketing program, exhibiting will result in a large investment with no real return.

There are as many philosophies of trade show exhibiting as there are companies exhibiting. Go to any trade show and you'll see every different approach possible being used to drag attendees into booths. As you meander through the average trade show, you'll see one exhibit that cost tens of thousands next to another company with their logo stapled to the backdrop curtains. Further down the aisle will be someone who sprung for the fake Persian carpet and soft leather sofas accented by a fountain and soft music. They are hoping their booth will be an inviting oasis to weary passersby. Another earnest hopeful rented a popcorn machine to snare customers with the smells and sounds of popping corn. Premiums are a common lure. You'll be offered anything from glow in the dark yo-yos to your business cards laminated into luggage tags.

Who has the most successful exhibit? The answer is the exhibitor who arrived at the show with a game plan for obtaining leads. Here's the secret of trade show success: It's human behavior.

When someone comes into your booth, whether for a bag of popcorn or to talk about your products, immediately qualify them. You must determine if they are a legitimate prospect immediately. If they are prospects, start a conversation with them. If they are not, give them their popcorn and get rid of them.

Train your staff to identify a potential customer in less than 30 seconds – trust me this is possible. If someone is not a prospective client, they are taking up space that a prospect should occupy. Do not miss out on three prospects who pass by while someone who cannot possibly buy from you sits on your sofa, eats you popcorn, and takes up your time.

Premiums as draws seldom achieve the results you want. Someone who comes into your booth only for the key chain is more likely someone's spouse wandering the show floor in search of trinkets. People who are genuinely interested in what you have to offer will want the opportunity to talk with you. Make your products and their benefits crystal clear to passersby in the aisle. Put on a live demonstration. Schedule seminars right in your booth. Make prospects' entry into your booth educational and worth their time. Show how to solve a problem using your products and services.

Here are some procedures to follow in planning and exhibiting at a trade show to make the entire experience as profitable as possible.

Get to the right ones – A significant factor in whether you return with the right leads is whether the people you want to sell to are even at the show. Before signing up for a trade show, look over lists of attendees from last year's show. If they don't match your client demographics, don't go. Take this a step further and call some of the attendees from the last show to ask them how they liked the show and if they are attending this year. If most are not, you've spotted a trend. Be warned away before you pay to set up a booth and talk to the other exhibitors because attendance was down this year.

Get on the seminar program – As a speaker, you'll receive well over 20 times the exposure as from the best booth on the floor. Give a seminar session – it not only gives you a full hour to sell to prospects, it gives you credibility as an expert. Invite people with questions to visit your booth afterwards.

Get their mailing list – After the show, you want a complete mailing list of all attendees. Many Trade Show organizers are reluctant to provide this. The time to negotiate this is before you pony up your bucks for the exhibit booth. Include a disk of all registrants in your agreement to exhibit. Most organizers will agree to provide you with the list if you bargain for it when agreeing to take space.

Get Prepared – What specific information do you need from attendees? A lot of exhibitors use a fish bowl for people to drop their business cards – this only gives you a mailing list of the people who were at the show. You're already getting that from the organizers. You need the answers to 5 – 8 specific questions from every prospective client. Decide what they are and make up a questionnaire.

Get Aggressive – Throwing people out of an exhibit booth seems counter productive to most people. After all, you are there to meet people, aren't you? The answer is "No." This is not a social occasion. This is a very expensive business investment. To make it pay off, you must concentrate on people who are prospective customers. Move people out of your booth (tactfully and politely) if they are not prospects.

Finally, after the show, **Get Busy**. Get on the phone and follow-up. If the contact you met in your booth is not the decision-maker, use them to make an introduction. Virtually no one is going to buy from you at the trade show. The sale is going to be made after you all go back to your businesses.

Trade Shows can be enormously successful. They put you in personal contact with people who can and should be customers. By asking the right questions, you obtain contact and buying information you will need to sell to them after the show. And most important, trade shows help you identify the decision maker. Use trade shows effectively and they can be well worth the cost. If you don't use them effectively, you'll only give away a lot of glow in the dark yo-yo's.

Need Help?
Look in the Appendix for a Sample Trade Show Prospect Form.

How to Choose an Advertising Agency

Choosing the right advertising agency may be the most difficult choice a manager makes. Choosing the right agency and establishing the right relationship with them can increase your market share dramatically. Choosing the wrong one will only make you frustrated and can waste a great deal of money. There are several things you can do to increase your chances of making the right selection.

An agency that is right for one company may be totally wrong for another. So it is your job to select the right one based on your company and your needs. Before you start calling every agency in the phone book though, you need to do some extensive homework.

Start by writing out in depth answers to the following:

- What is your advertising/marketing budget for the next two years

- What are your growth goals for the next two years

- What are your marketing challenges

- Who is your competition – why are you better than they are

- What marketing have you tried in the past – how well has each program worked

- What are the steps to a sale for your products and services

- What additional markets should you be reaching

Now write out a complete description of your company, your culture, your products and services, and who your clients are. When all this is done, you are ready to start the selection process.

Write a letter to every potential firm listed in the Yellow Pages. Find these firms under Ad Agencies, Public Relations, and Marketing Consultants. If the number of firms is large, you can save a bit on postage by calling each one and asking if they do your kind of work and are they accepting new clients.

In your letter, include a brief explanation of the kind of company you are, your products and services, and your advertising/marketing budget. Explain a little about your marketing challenges and ask them if they would like to work with you. If they would like to be considered, send them the entire package.

Send a schedule with the package. Items on the schedule will be:

- Initial interviews by [date]

- Presentations completed by [date]

- Follow up presentations by [date]

- Selection by [date]

- Begin work on [date]

When the companies start making presentations, use a method of evaluation that quantifies their capability. Rate each company numerically on each of the following:

- How well do they understand your industry

- How well do they understand your products and services

- How well do they understand your client universe

- How well do they understand your company

- How creative are they

- How thorough is their program

- Do they meet your marketing challenges

- Will their programs be effective

- Will their programs fit within your budget

- What will the working relationship be with the consulting firm

- Are they enjoyable to work with

Now you should have a mathematical numbering scale that identifies one winner, or at least narrows it down. Before making a final choice, call their references, especially those in similar industries! Make sure their clients are glowing and positive about the increased sales the agency has brought them.

This system will help you find the exact right ad agency to help you reach your sales goals. Hire them and own the market.

How to be a Speaker at Trade Shows

Have you ever spent a small fortune to exhibit at a trade show only to find your fiercest competitor was on the program? You spent the money and he got the recognition!

Speaking at trade shows and seminars is an outstanding way to gain recognition, exposure, and third party credibility. But if you're waiting to be called, get ready to continue watching your competitors get all the glory.

Organizers of seminars typically don't call you to speak. In most cases, you have to call them. Before you reach for the phone though, do some advance preparation. Prepare an informational package that includes the following:

1. A Resume/biography - list your education, accomplishments, significant work history in your field, and organization memberships.

2. A professional photo of yourself. Don't monkey around with a Polaroid, this is serious business and it demands a serious photo. Go to a professional

photographer and have it done right. Put your name, company, and phone number on the back of the photos.

3. Prepare a list of the subjects you can present. The list should include the topic with short explanation of content and most important the benefits that will be derived by someone listening to your talk. "How To" talks are very popular.

4. A description of your company including background, products and services, and list of major clients, especially if your clients are easily recognizable names such as IBM or Nike.

Does this sound like shameless self promotion? It is. However, it is necessary to be included on a speaking program. Conference organizers need this information to do their job. You are providing them with the facts so they can ascertain your credentials, pick the topic that balances their program, and include you in their written program and advertising materials for the seminar. By making it easy for them to include you on their program, they are much more likely to do so.

Once your homework is complete, start calling organizers of conferences in your industry. They start preparing for these a year in advance so start early. Ask the theme of their next conference. Tailor your topic list to match their theme and send off a kit.

Once you are listed as a speaker on the program, leverage the event with the following:

1. Send a Press Release telling about your presentation to the local and industry newspapers and journals (include your photo – aren't you glad you had good ones taken?)

2. Send invitations to your talk to your prime list of potential clients – even if they don't attend, you've

planted the image of "Expert Credentials" in their minds.

3. Send copies of the newspaper articles about your presentation to your list of prospects after the event. Offer to send copies of the talk if they didn't attend the conference.

People who organize conferences are looking for qualified, capable speakers. By demonstrating that you know your stuff and are easy to work with, you will sky rocket to the top of their list of favorite speakers.

One final note, make your presentations interesting as well as informative. Many people assume that since their content is valuable, they don't have to worry about presentation. This is wrong. Great content won't save you from being boring. Make your talk interesting so your audience will get out of it all that you put into creating it.

The World's Best Marketing Plan

How much should the World's Best Marketing Plan cost to implement?

Good marketing, marketing that is effective, does not have to cost a lot of money. In many cases, it doesn't even have to cost any money. Consider the following true example of one of the most cost effective marketing programs I've ever seen. As you read it, keep track of the accumulated implementation costs.

One day I telephoned a taxi to take me to the airport. When it arrived, the taxi driver came right up to my door rather than blow his horn in the driveway. He introduced himself as Charles and grabbed my suitcase from the foyer to carry it to his car. As I followed him out to the car, he held open the back door and ushered me into his 4 year old Chevrolet as if it were a new Rolls. A fresh cup of coffee was waiting for me along with today's Washington Post, neatly folded on the seat (Are you counting the cost? We're up to about 50 cents – Charles brews the coffee at home and brings it in the giant thermos).

As he drove me to the airport, he asked about my business. He asked about the trip I was taking. He asked me when I was returning. He offered to meet my flight when I came back so I wouldn't have to wait in line for a taxi. He wrote down my return flight number and gave me his business card. He asked me to call him if there were any change in my schedule.

When I returned from the trip, he was standing there waiting for me at the baggage claim area. He pointed to the car and told me to give him my baggage claim check. The coffee and paper were waiting for me again (total marketing cost now is up to about $1, although since the paper was reused from customer to customer we probably should not count it). As Charles drove me home, he asked about my next trip. He also asked if I would like him to pick me up. I said yes. He once again gave me his business card and once again told me to call him if there were any changes to my schedule. He hand wrote his home number on the card and told me to call him night or day if an unexpected trip came up or I just needed a driver for around town trips. He explained that many of his clients used him to drive them to business meetings, especially to DC where parking could take up a great deal of valuable time. He asked me when my next trip to DC was and wondered if I wanted him to drive me as a test to see if I liked it. Of course, I said yes.

That was two years ago. Since then I have had my own personal taxi driver. I call Charles for every trip to the airport and most trips to DC. There's always a cup of coffee and the paper waiting for me when he ushers me into his cab. I've used him when traveling around town with clients and found our ability to talk without thinking about driving or parking to be much more productive. Needless to say, I tip Charles about 4 times what I would any other taxi driver and on my last trip with a business associate, my associate handed Charles a larger tip than I had already given him, she was so impressed with the service – coffee goes a long way with her.

Charles never graduated from high school. He grew up in inner city DC and quit school to help support his family when he was 15. With no real education he now makes about double what other taxi drivers make. Without an MBA, he developed a marketing plan with a cost return ratio that most large corporations would kill for. Why is his marketing plan so effective?

There are several reasons:

1. He develops a relationship with each client. He makes you feel like he is YOUR taxi driver. Once that relationship is rooted, you feel disloyal riding in a taxi driven by anyone else.

2. He gets instant returns on his direct marketing costs. His tip far exceeds the amount he spends on coffee and newspaper for each client.

3. He stands out from his competition.

4. He gets maximum repeat business from his clients.

5. He conducts add-on selling in ways that point out additional services (driver for DC trips as well as airport shuttle).

6. He uses a positive sales approach without the customer ever feeling like he's being "sold to."

I once asked Charles how he developed his system of dealing with clients. He told me he learned it from a clothing salesman who used to call him at home every time a new shipment came in or they were having a special sale. "I was struggling for fares like every other cab driver and barely getting by. One day it occurred to me that I could use the same system as that pants salesman was doing with me. Now, I make twice what other drivers do. I have customers call the cab company and ask for me, and I enjoy every minute of every day as I drive fine folks like you around."

What can we learn from Charles? First and foremost, an effective marketing program does not need to cost a lot. It doesn't even need to cost anything.

Second, personal service sells, especially in an environment where the expected level of personal service is very low. This applies to most industries.

Finally, we learn that developing a relationship with your clients pays off big time. Understanding your clients needs and finding ways to help meet them will do a lot for the client relationship. This in turn does a lot for your revenue stream. Use the low cost stuff to increase the big return stuff.

Marketing can be very costly. It also can be very cost effective. The next time you're wondering how to increase sales, remember Charles calling me at home to ask when my next trip was going to be and offering to pick me up. Good marketing is really that simple.

Are You Creative?

Are you creative? Does a clean sheet of paper hold no threat to you? Can you come up with a unique marketing idea guaranteed to be memorable? Or do you quiver at the thought of having to think of unique ideas and leave the creativity to someone else?

Most people do not consider themselves creative. They consider creativity to be something that strikes certain people at birth. It's like blue eyes, you either get it or you don't. Yet, creativity is the very key to making your business successful. It is where you stand out from your competition.   It's   how   you   make   your   business remembered in your client's eyes. And most important, it's how you get the most bang for the buck in your advertising.

So, if you're not born creative, how do you come up with the ideas? Here is the real secret to creativity – it's far less inspiration from above than it is hard work. And it's something anyone can do, even if you don't have a creative corpuscle in your blood stream.

The best creativity is the product of brainstorming. The power of several minds can develop solutions where one mind will bog down. Here's how you use creative brainstorming to achieve success:

Assemble a Creative Council. Round up a mix of people whose judgment and opinions you respect. Ideally include staff members, customers, and outsiders. Five to seven people is an ideal size to stimulate ideas without being too unwieldy to make progress.

Compensate people for their participation on the Council so they'll take it seriously and show up for meetings. Create a written agreement that spells out what you expect of each member of the Council. Have the non-employees sign a non-disclosure agreement to prevent any compromise of your trade secrets.

Here the ingredients for your Creative Council:

Be Positive – regardless of how ridiculous or outlandish an idea is when it is presented, it must be accepted and discussed without criticism. This is vital to the free flow of creative juices. Throughout history, virtually every revolutionary idea from the steamboat to the television was dismissed as ridiculous when first presented. Success has come to those who did something while others were saying it was impossible.

Bounce Off – real creativity happens when everyone is talking at once. One person's idea sparks a fire in someone else's mind. Their embers trigger explosion in a third person, and so on. Creativity is raucous. When it happens, feed it rather than cut it off.

Nothing is Sacred – it's very tempting hold some cows too sacred for consideration. Change is a pretty scary thing. Relax. True creativity demands everything is up for grabs. Identifying any thing as off limits prevents true consideration of every option. Encourage everyone to question everything.

Stretch and Stretch – stretch the envelope. The assumption is that something can't be done if no one has done it before. Perhaps they just haven't thought of it yet. True creativity is leading, not following.

Add a Dash of Structure - too much structure will stifle the explosion of ideas. Too little structure will end up in only eating the pizza and going home with nothing accomplished. Adjust the process to the point where you're effective without being stifling. Have a printed agenda with goals clearly spelled out.

Creative brainstorming can achieve the impossible. It can solve problems you have agonized over for years. It can create new ideas for your marketing strategy. It can increase customer satisfaction. It can increase efficiency.

Assemble a Creative Council. You'll be amazed at how creative you are.

How to Use Direct Mail Effectively

You've no doubt heard that direct mail only brings a 2% return rate? If so, you're probably reluctant to try it as a lead generator.

If so, I've got bad news for you -- the 2% return rate is an average – many direct mail projects yield much less than that. I've done direct mail programs that resulted in 2 hundredths of a percent return rate (.0002). Believe it or not, the client was quite satisfied with those results.

Direct mail works. It works very well. If it didn't, you wouldn't be plowing though piles of the debris on your desk every day. Even though you may Frisbee the majority of your mail into the trash each day (how do you think it got the name Junk Mail?) without a glimmer of curiosity of contents, enough people buy as a result of direct mail that it can be very cost effective.

There are definitive ways to increase the effectiveness of a direct mail campaign. Here are five main elements to the success of a direct mail campaign:

1. The List -- You should already have on your computer a mailing list of "HOT" prospects. Supplement this with additional names. You can get these from list brokers, magazines (who sell their subscriber lists), the phone book.

2. The Piece – The range of potential mail pieces is endless. You can send full color flyers; postcards; multi-part pieces; letters, brochures, you name it. And that's just the range of printed materials. You can also mail items like Frisbees, candy jars, seed packets. Make the Crime fit the Punishment -- create a piece that matches your industry.

3. The Message – What you say is vital. Make sure your message is simple, quick, and leads to a direct response by your audience. Responding must be easy. Print your phone number, fax number, and e-mail address large and bold. If you use a response card, make sure your address and phone number is still on the piece after the card is torn off.

4. Repetition - If you were advertising on the radio you wouldn't hesitate to air the same audio spot 30 - 60 times a week. Yet, people send out one mail piece and wonder where the sales are. Repetition is just as important in direct mail. Mail something to your list 8 - 10 times per year. One way to save on printing costs is to print 3 mailings worth at a time (thus saving per piece printing costs). Then mail that piece every other month – mix it in with other pieces.

5. Follow-up – After you mail a piece, call them. Divide your list of names among the sales staff and get on the phone. You can increase direct mail effectiveness 10 fold with a follow-up phone call.

Done right, direct mail can and will be a cost-effective method of bringing in sales. Unlike mass media, it reaches exactly the people you want to reach when you want to reach them. Used correctly, direct mail can be an important part of a successful marketing campaign. Be creative, and you'll blow the pants off the 2% average return.

Are We Having Fun Yet?

The client had flown in from Florida. We were enroute back to the airport. As we passed a restaurant near my office, she asked, "Do you ever eat there?"

"No," I answered. "I went a couple times, but never went back."

"Why not? It looks like a good place to eat." She was puzzled.

"It wasn't fun," was my reply.

After depositing the client at the friendly skies place, I got thinking about that restaurant and their lack of customer keeping ability, at least as far as I was concerned. There was nothing really wrong with it. The food was good, the service was okay. But I did not continue as a customer. In fact now when considering someplace to eat, they never even pop up on the landscape.

They didn't ring my bell. And because they don't make dining with them a memorable and enjoyable experience, I don't go there.

Is it fun to do business with your company? One of the most critical elements you can build into your marketing program is the Enjoyment Factor. How much do customers enjoy doing business with you? Is your fun quotient as high as it could be?

Let's assume you're doing at least an okay job creating and delivering your products. Your staff is well trained. People like the stuff you sell. You think you've done everything you can to be successful. Yet without a significant Enjoyment Factor, business will never be as good as it could be.

Think of the worst seminar you ever attended. Recall the agony of fidgeting in your seat while enduring a speaker who simply read his material. You checked your watch every hour and found only 2 minutes had passed. You looked around and your fellow attendees were equally miserable. The speaker was knowledgeable and capable. But his delivery was B O O O O R I N G............. When it finally ended, you couldn't wait to get out of the room.

Now think about the best speaker you ever heard. He or she was entertaining, creative, engaging, and humorous. Time flew by as you listened and you were somewhat disappointed when they concluded. Which speaker was better informed or provided more critical information?

Likely the boring speaker had more content in his speech. But because the delivery was so painful, you got more out of the entertaining speaker's presentation. Delivery is critical. How you present something is as important to success as what you present.

No matter what your product or service, the decision to purchase from you is always made by people. IBM may be your client, but it's IBM employees who make the purchase decisions. The more you make their experience with you enjoyable, the more likelihood of them calling you rather than your competitors.

Your clients have mortgages to pay. Their kids need new braces. They have to leave work early to go to a PTA meeting. Ordering more computer supplies is not going to brighten their life. So put a song in their heart when they do business with you. Do something funny, or entertaining, or motivating. You will be first choice the next time they need more copy paper.

Here's a quick test to determine the Enjoyment Factor for your business. Take it honestly and keep track of your score.

Hello, welcome to Acme Bowling Balls – Put this book down and call your own company. Go on you know the number. How is the greeting?

❑ Wow, made my day go better just listening to it

5 points

❑ When you've talked to one receptionist you've talked to them all

0 points

❑ I think the receptionist has been dead for 3 weeks

-5 points

Printed Stuff – Now grab your corporate brochure or catalogue and read it – all of it! How was it?

❑ Riveting – I turned down an invitation to play golf so I could finish

5 points

❑ It was okay -- I fell asleep a couple times trying to get through it

0 points

❑ I think whoever wrote the brochure has been dead for 3 weeks

-5 points

Service – Go to wherever you serve people and time how long people have to wait:.

- ❏ People were served promptly and left with a smile

  5 points

- ❏ People had to wait quite a while but they didn't seem to mind

  0 points

- ❏ We may have a customer who has been dead for 3 weeks

  -5 points

Creative R Us – Get in your car and drive to a competitor. Buy something. What's the difference between your store and theirs?

- ❏ We are much more fun to shop with

  5 points

- ❏ We are mediocre, but they're more mediocre

  0 points

- ❏ I'd rather shop with them

  -5 points

Add up your score. If your total score is negative, check and see if you've been dead for 3 weeks. If not, get to work.

The Enjoyment Factor is how you differentiate your business from the competitors. If you sell the same products at close to the same prices, in what other ways will customers tell you from your competitors, by the color of your logo? Making buying from you enjoyable will generate immediate increases in sales usually with little or no increase of expenses. Ultimately, it's probably the most cost-effective marketing program you can implement.

Well guess I'll go to lunch now. Wonder if that restaurant has added any exiting menu items?

How good is a good excuse?

Way back in high school, I managed an ice cream store for a summer job. One Friday afternoon, as I unpacked a shipment of supplies ordered in for the weekend rush, I realized no napkins were in the delivery. I checked to verify I had actually ordered the napkins, then shrugged and figured, "I did what I could."

It was a hot sticky weekend – just the kind of weather to bring long lines of eager faces to an ice cream store. The napkin holders ran dry Saturday morning. The rest of the weekend consisted of explaining why the napkin holders were empty to frustrated, messy customers. I remember going in great detail to one customer just how I had ordered the napkins and through no fault of my own, they just weren't on Friday's delivery. "What else could I do?" was left unsaid but clearly implied. This mother watching ice cream dripping down her son's shirt on that hot summer's day, was clearly unimpressed. I was tempted to explain it all again so she would understand how much I had done to get those pesky napkins.

As I look back now, I was pretty naïve. I actually thought customers would be proud of me for trying so hard to do the right thing. I had done my best to get the napkins and the fact that the napkin dispensers were empty was not because of poor management on my part. But in reality, I hadn't done everything I could. Going to the supermarket and buying regular table napkins never occurred to me. I was so sure my customers would accept a good excuse in lieu of good performance, I never took the extra steps to actually provide performance.

I thought about my youthful management clumsiness the other day when I called the computer store to inquire about the state of repairs on my new laptop computer. I was admittedly already a bit irritated since it had already been in their service shop more than it had been on my desk since I bought it.

After I endured their "hard rock on hold" phone system for a while, a real person came on the line. He quite proudly explained that he had done all he could by ordering the part. He told me the dates he sent the order to the manufacturer and was clearly of the opinion that I would share his belief that we were discussing a job well done here. I asked if he had called the manufacturer to follow-up. He had not, but he was willing to "Go the extra mile" and call. He explained to me that all he could do was ask them for an ETA, which may be several more weeks. I explained to him that I didn't lay out $1600 to have my computer sitting in their repair shop and I thought they could do a great deal more than simply inquire about an ETA. He was explaining the reason why I didn't have my computer. I wasn't interested in explanations. I wanted performance.

It was another napkin crisis. The tech support person thought I would be happy with all he had done on my behalf. I simply wanted my computer back. I had bought it to use, not to have it lay on their shelves. He thought, as I had so long ago, that a good excuse was equivalent to good performance. I felt, exactly as that mother had back then, that good performance is the only equivalence.

Customers frequently have a different definition of exceptional performance than you do. Often, they expect more than you are delivering. When problems arise, the difference in expectations grows exponentially. How can you deliver the performance your clients expect and still keep your sanity as well as your business? Here are a few hints.

- Set expectations lower than you know you will deliver. Most customer expectations are created by sales people. In order to get the sale, sales people will promise things based on a "Best Case" scenario. Then delivery is made with all the excuses to explain why you didn't meet the deadlines (or quality or quantity or price or ....) the customer expected. Rather than promise the best case, promise the worst case – knowing all along that you'll beat it.

- Keep the customer in the loop. If your process takes more than a few times from order to delivery, communicate with the customer with periodic updates. Don't let them feel abandoned. Send them a postcard telling the status of their order. Call them to say you just put their job into final processing and it will be delivered tomorrow. Part of my frustration with the computer repair was not knowing what was going on. They took the computer and I never heard from them again. If there are going to be delays, let the customer know as soon as you know.

- When there is a problem, do everything you can to fix it quickly. Customers are usually ready to work with you if you let them.

- Ultimately do everything you can to prevent the need for an excuse in the first place. Train your staff that excuses are not equivalent to performance. Always look for that better way to meet the customer's expectations.

- Some things, like napkins in an ice cream store are basic. Identify the basics in your operation and make sure that no matter what, they will be on hand, ready for use when customers need them.

Making excuses is much less obvious now as adults than when we tried to explain why we didn't finish our homework to our 9th grade teacher. But explanations are caused by failure to deliver, whether we're talking about homework or computers.

Work to eliminate excuses from your dealing with customers. Make it a point of never having to offer one instead of performing. And when you do, remember the empty napkin dispensers with ice cream dripping down the little boy's shirt. Excuses are no match for performance!

Do you use your products?

It was near the end of the day and I needed to transfer funds before the bank closed in 30 minutes. I decided to use PC Banking to save the trip to the bank. As the computers connected, a message flashed saying a software update was going to download. I didn't want new software, but no one asked me. I was getting new software whether I wanted it or not.

I drummed my fingers while the graphs gradually filled. The computer signed off with instructions to connect again. More minutes slipped by. I attempted to sign on again. No dice. The update had erased my Account Number. I could not sign on without it. I had no idea what it might be. I entered my checking account number. Wrong! I looked through the PC Banking manual. No help. More minutes slipped by. It was too short to be my social security number. I considered jumping in the car and driving to the bank.

I called my branch. To my stunned astonishment, no one, including the branch manager knew any thing about their PC banking system. She gave me tech support's number. PC Banking was clearly not very important to the staff of the branch. My funds did not get transferred by the end of the day.

This particular bank is known for its customer friendly procedures. What went wrong? The answer is very simple – they don't use their own services. When a software gremlin glitch popped up, they didn't know about it.

Do you use your products and services? Do you have a company policy that requires every employee to use company products and services in the same way that customers do? You should.

Most companies give employee discounts to encourage them to shop at their business. However if employees circumvent normal shopping channels in doing business with you, they aren't seeing your business as a customer would. My bank gives checking accounts free to their employees. That brings employees not one bit closer to understanding the customer's perspective. Bank employees don't have to stand in line on their lunch hour to get their paycheck cashed. They don't have to sit and wait for the loan officer. And they clearly don't have to use PC Banking to get information about their own accounts.

If using your own products is unrealistic, watch your customers use them. Follow them back to their office and see your products in their environment. Set up an advisory panel of customers to increase communication and ultimately customer satisfaction.

Keeping tabs on your products and services by using them yourself has always been critical. Now, with the advent of so many technical devices, from email to voice mail, it is even more vital that you test and monitor your systems from the customer's perspective. As technology allows us to communicate without actually talking to someone, following a policy of zealously monitoring your products and services is even more vital. Test every system before inflicting it on your clients. It's a whole lot cheaper than trying to fix it later.

Your customers see your products and services from the outside in, you see them from the inside out. Make sure the two views are the same.

Who Pays for Your Mistakes?

You try to do right by your customers. You have policies dictating customer friendly policies and possibly even have written policies telling what to do if there is a problem. But sometimes it seems impossible to make everyone happy. Making customers happy is not a simple matter. You can't make any money letting customers walk all over you – for example allowing someone to return a dress after they wore it to the prom. Some customers want more than you think they deserve, others are clearly out to take advantage of you. And finally there are the times when you just plain screw up. When a mistake happens, who pays for it?

Here are 2 true customer episodes. Both happened to people I know. As you read each one, think about how, as a manager, you would handle a similar situation in your business.

Situation I

The customer is purchasing wallpaper. The in-store designer has measured the rooms in his house and picked out the wallpaper. The customer loves her suggestions and says, "We'll take it all." He stands, checkbook in hand waiting while the designer enters numbers into a calculator to add up the cost of the order. After several minutes, she announces a total of $541.60. The customer starts writing out the check. She advises him that he needs to pay only half up front, but he waves his hand and says he wants to pay everything at once and get it over with. Besides, he laughs, he trusts them.

The next day the customer finds a message on his answering machine saying the designer made a mistake in adding up his total and it should have come to $576.60. Would he please bring in the additional $35 as soon as possible?

Situation II

She is a new Senior Vice President for a large company. She flies home every weekend as part of her transition to the job. Her company pays for the flights. She calls the company's travel agent and books a flight as she has done several times. She pays no attention to the itinerary when it arrives from the travel agent. The morning of her departure though, she notices the return flight is booked for 3 weeks later, not the end of the weekend. She calls the travel agency. They agree to change the flight booking but want to bill the $75 airline change fee to the company. The customer is adamant that the error is the travel agent's and no bill should be issued. They argue that even if the error was theirs in the first place, the customer should have looked at the itinerary and ticket before the last minute. She says they should have known that she wouldn't be gone for 3 weeks from a new job.

What would you have done in each of these situations? These examples have several things in common. Each represents money the company is faced with paying to remedy their own mistake. In the case of the travel agent, the amount in question far exceeds their profit from the sale. Also common is the fact that the mistake was clearly the company's. Yet, each company had their defenses up at the start.

The wallpaper company felt the customer should pay the correct amount due regardless of math errors. The travel agency gets 4 or 5 calls a day from people who insist they told them a different departure or return date and want the agency to stand behind the change.

Since these were real life situations, I can tell you the actual outcome of each one. They have one more thing in common, each one lost the customer. The wallpaper customer refused to pay the $35 and demanded they live up to the original agreement. They did, the wallpaper was delivered with a frosty crispness. The buyer took his order, refused to ever do business with them again, and told every one of his friends the story.

The Senior Vice President it turns out was the person in charge of which travel agency the company used. She pulled their corporate travel business and gave it to another agency. The cost of their mistake turned out to by far higher than just $75.

Customers have high expectations. Can you meet them? If you don't, customers will take their business to someone who will. As the bumper sticker says, 'Mistakes Happen.' When they do, don't let them cost you the customer or the business. Work to ensure mistakes happen as seldom as possible. When they do, make sure they are handled professionally and with respect.

Mistakes happen. Who pays for them? You do, in every case.

Cleaning up the hard drive

It's suddenly year-end. I blinked in July and the next thing I know it's Christmas. Time for the annual New Year Clean Office binge. I pull out the trashcan and start flinging into it everything that has now been overcome by events. Invitations to meetings that happened months ago hit first. Ads for software I was considering but the sale ended in August go next. The articles and newsletters I am still planning to read get moved from the In Box to a "Suspense" file. They'll sit there until Clean Office day extends to the file cabinets as well. More likely will buy new file cabinets first.

I clean up the electronic files from my computer hard drive as well. As I get to the "Marketing Guy Column" directory, several partly done articles are there, waiting for more work. The reason they weren't finished was always the same. Not enough words. They were great ideas but I couldn't stretch them to 950 words.

So here is a year end compilation of all those ideas. Please consider each one as if it were a full column – it'll save us both time and me computer space.

Reduce the procedures – do you have procedures that slow down or prevent sales? I thought of this while standing at a cash register waiting to have a $103 check approved. Their policy was clogging up the works - - a manager has to approve checks over $100. No manager was in sight. Customers, cashiers, staff all stood around fidgeting. I offered to give them $5 in cash to bring the check below the $100 threshold. We could all get on with our lives. No dice. Later I offered to give them the whole $103 in cash. No can do. Once a check is rung it stays rung. While I can understand the need for check approval, this system was costing the store revenues. Customers left. I wanted to leave. A manager was finally tracked down and brought to the register. She barely looked at me before initialing the check. The cash register began ringing again. But the delay was costly. Make sure your policies are as transparent as possible to your customers. And implement them in ways that do not slow the flow of dollars into the till.

Math R Us – Carol and I are members of a boating organization that has a chain of retail stores. I headed into their store the other day carrying a return item as well as coupons and discount certificates they had sent us. The math involved in entering all this into the electronic cash register was clearly beyond the capability of the cashier. He fumbled along for a while and then announced that I owed them $54.21, the number displayed on the register. I wrote out a check and he handed me the cash register receipt. I checked the receipt and realized he had not given me credit for a $20 store coupon. He returned my check and started the ringing up process from scratch. At the end of the new calculation, he now announced that they owed me $8.38, which he cheerfully took from the register and gave to me. In truth I owed them $34.21, the original figure less $20. But I was too tired to argue or worse, watch him grind through the whole process one more time. The customers behind me would have killed me. This store lost $40 in income (translate profits) from this one sale because of their inability to calculate their own discounts. If you have sales or discounts, keep them simple and make sure your staff can do the math.

Give us your list – How often have you wandered into one of these cavernous super stores carrying a list of items you need and then left without finding all the stuff you intended to buy? If you manage a retail store, take the customer's list when they come through the door and find everything for them. Not only does this ensure that you sell them everything they came in for, it also helps you increase sales as you suggest products to go with the items on their list.

Use Your Friends – Do you find a need to bounce new ideas around with someone. Use your friends. Call a business associate and ask him or her to go over concepts you are considering. Bring summaries of each concept and the peripheral information they will need to know to the meeting. Articulate the questions you want answered. You'll find a great deal of useful conversation to help crystallize your thoughts. Business people can provide the perspective you need because they've "been there." Take them for drinks afterwards.

It Started With the Clocks – Our health club started cutting costs by not buying new batteries for the clocks on the wall. Next they cut the budget for new equipment. Instructors followed. Soon they were scrambling to replace members who had quit because of the decline in services. When you make budget cuts, do them in ways that don't translate to reduced services for your clients or you will soon be making cuts to compensate for your reduced revenues. Find ways of cutting expenses that the client never sees, such as better purchasing, more efficient scheduling, and better management.

Be A Customer First – The best marketing ideas come from your own experiences as a customer. Whenever you buy something, look at what the vendor does well or poorly. Translate those to your own business. Industry does not matter. If you are irritated that your bill from the Cable Company was screwed up, the customers at your law firm will be no less frustrated when your invoice to them is wrong. If you seethed at waiting in an uncomfortable, messy lounge while your car was being serviced, give your customers comfortable sofas to sit on. When you are particularly impressed with a company's service, find ways to emulate them in your own business. If you find a unique promotion concept in another industry, see if it can translate over to your business. Cross industry applications can be very successful.

Wow! My desk is clean, the computer drive has more space, and I don't have to work any more on stretching these articles. We'll have all new topics next year. From our house to yours, we wish you all the very best of holidays and the most prosperous of New Years. May you and your family enjoy all the warmth and joy of this holiday season.

New Year's Resolutions

Okay - you've decided to lose 15 pounds, spend more time with your family and get better at golf next year. How about your business? Do you have any resolutions to make your business more successful? Here are 10 business resolutions you can make that you can implement immediately. No matter how successful you are, these will make you even more successful in the coming year.

1. Call 5 customers. Ask them what they like about doing business with you..... and ask them what they don't like. Ask them how you can improve your services to them and also what new products or services you could offer them. Listen very carefully to their answers and be ready to ask specific additional questions about any points that they bring up. Be sure to include a question like, "What would you do differently if you ran my company?"

2. Read a chapter in Alice in Wonderland. We all get too bogged down in the concrete of reality.... do something that stretches your imagination. I keep several whimsical books on my bookshelf as an

antidote for spending too long staring at a computer screen. A flow of ideas is usually enhanced by turning away from the subject at hand, not by concentrating on it more intensely.

Take 5 of your employees to lunch one at a time. Ask them what the company could be doing better, what additional tools they need to do their jobs better, what additional services and products the company should offer. You'll be surprised at how much they can tell you. Consultants frequently come in to a company, accept a nice retainer, and submit a report that does nothing more than present the ideas employees told the consultant. You can skip the consultant -- ask your employees yourself.

3. Read a chapter in the Bible, Koran, or Talmud. Keep in touch with your core values throughout the year. It will make you a better person and manager. What you believe in is what you are. And your company is a direct extension of you. Stay tuned to your inner self and keep what's important to you at the forefront of your mind.

4. Turn your desk around. Face a new way, you'll see things differently. It's amazing how effectively this minor change will generate major changes. Change the view from your desk, then change the scenery. Take down the 20-year-old photos of your kids growing up -- get some recent ones of your grandchildren. Change the wallpaper or even the furniture. If you continue to look at everything the same way, you'll likely have the same solutions to the same problems. Make some changes -- get a different perspective.

5. Leaf through the yellow pages or a business directory and find at least one new industry group to market your products or services to. There are additional industry groups that your product will

match with minimum modifications. Find a new target industry and develop a marketing strategy to go get them this year.

6. Shop one competitor. What are they doing that you could do better? What could you improve on in customer service? Test them on something that you don't think you're company does well and see how they handle it.

7. Offer every employee $100 in return for submitting a written new idea. Pick the best 5 and try them regardless of how successful they are likely to be. Your people have good ideas and will offer them when you encourage them to.

8. Have a friend call in to your company and order or buy something. Listen in to the phone call. Shopping yourself may be one of the most effective marketing tools ever invented. Look at your business from the outside rather than from the inside. You'll be amazed at how much you will learn from putting yourself in the customer's shoes.

9. Go to a Jackie Chan movie and come out with 3 new ideas to bury your competition. Coming in second is the first way of losing. Determine to come out number one, every time. The New Year is a good time to decide to move significantly ahead of the competition and surpass your own best efforts.

These are actions that will substantially increase your company's effectiveness during the coming year. Do them all and you'll be amazed at what a good year next year will be.

Appendix – Sample Forms

Preventing "May I Help You"

Here are 20 greetings you can use to increase sales. Every one works better than "May I Help You" as a method of engaging a prospect into conversation when they enter a retail store. While many are specialized for a specific industry, most can be adapted to your situation and will work very well.

1. Welcome to Fisher Autos.

2. Those would look great on you

3. Have you seen our latest shipment of sweaters?

4. Are you shopping for yourself or a relative today?

5. Would you like to set those packages down?

6. What shall I show you today?

7. How do you do, my name is Leon Frank. Welcome to Acme Hardware.

8. Are you here for the sale?

9. Are you ready for the finest listening experience anywhere? Wait until you hear our new car stereos.

10. Are you here for the new spring line?

11. Are you here for our selection of ....?

12. Give me your shopping list. I'll help you find everything.

13. What a great outfit you're wearing. Are you shopping for something just as snazzy?

14. Are you familiar with our system of discounts?

15. Congratulations, you have just entered the finest men's store in Annapolis.

16. What would you like me to help you find?

17. What mood are you in today, Neil Diamond or The Boston Pops?

18. Would you like us to watch your children while you shop?

19. What can I show you today that we can have delivered and installed by the end of the week?

20. When was the last time you drove a brand new Mercury?

Special Bonus Option (this requires a special personality and the right circumstances, but can be a lot of fun):

21. Come in out of the cold, take your coat off, spend money, buy stuff, take it home, feel better.

Sales Force Comprehensive Outline

MC Solutions
Multimedia Sales Person

Personal Attributes

- Self Starter
- Extremely presentable
- Creative
- Positive personality
- Can work with a bunch of techies
- Can speak our language as well as the language of the boardroom
- Mature
- Easy nature
- Computer literate
- Can work well with a small team
- Leader
- Articulate
- Can travel 4 - 5 days per month

Business Attributes

- Can reach and talk with CEO's
- Can clearly explain Multimedia and its benefits
- Equally articulate over the phone and in person
- Works well with little supervision
- Will take ownership of the Multimedia sales department and run with it

- Will always try to exceed goals

- Proficient with Word, Excel, and Power Point

- Proficient with contact management software – preferably ACT!

- Can create and make effective sales presentations

- Has defined and tested selling skills

- Is knowledgeable about the multimedia industry – preferably with direct experience in the industry

Some familiarity or experience with as many as possible of the following fields:

- Computer based training

- Advertising

- Public Relations

- Corporate reports

- Corporate training

- Video production

- Production of commercials

Experienced in Trade Shows

Can give presentations and seminars to groups of 50 or more

Prefer some management experience

Prefer direct industry experience

Scope of Work

- Will be sole multimedia sales person

- Will essentially manage marketing budget including placement of ads and decisions about methods of marketing
- Will directly respond to all incoming sales leads
- To take ownership of each lead and follow-up with them until death
- To do follow-up phone calls, write follow-up letters, and make sales presentations (both in person and over the phone), and close the sale
- To enter the order into production, then interface with the customer throughout creation of multimedia presentation
- To make intermediate presentations to client as presentations are being created To bring back to technicians all changes suggested by customers Sales person will be only interface between technical and customer
- To develop creative sales promotion ideas
- To conduct periodic mailings to prospects
- To conduct periodic seminars for prospects and clients
- To represent MC at Trade Shows
- To grow business so we need to hire additional mm sales people As that happens, to be able to grow into the manger's function

Business Expectations

- To become proficient with MC products and services within 1 month

- To sign a major account (over $30,000) within the first 3 months

- To achieve a total of $300,000 in gross sales within the first year

- To be ready to hire additional sales people at the end of 1 year

- To make MC the renown leader in multimedia

- To establish a mailing list of over 1000 true prospective clients

Compensation Package

- Base Salary of $3000 per month

- Commission of 10% of gross revenues (paid as funds are received by MC)

- Bonus of 2% for every month when sales exceed $50,000

- Bonus of $5000 if sales goal of $300,000 is met in first year

Interview Sequence

1. Initial interview with Human Resources – analytical and personal aptitude tests will be given. HR will use rate applicants using a number scale of 1 – 10

2. Top 12 candidates will meet with President – he will reduce list to 6

3. They will be interviewed via telephone by CEO who will reduce list to 3

4. Final selection by heads of Marketing, Technical, and Production and President together

Time Frame

- Ads to go in paper for 2 weeks continuous starting 2/4
- Expect to start HR interviews by 2/25
- Complete president's interviews by 3/6
- Complete CEO interviews by 3/13
- Final decision by 3/20
- Start work on 4/6

Sample Sales Person Compensation Agreement

Acme Bowling Balls (ACME) employs_____Leon Frank____
(Associate) as Sales Associate according to the following
terms:

Scope of Work
Associate will work at least 40 hours per week from 9AM
until 6PM daily with 1 hour off for lunch. Associate is
expected to be at his desk at Acme unless traveling or
calling on clients.
Associate is responsible for the following:

- Receiving incoming sales call inquiries
- Creating and mailing responses to all phone inquiries
- All follow-up to potential customers via phone and mail
- Making In-person sales presentations both at Acme offices and at client's site
- Taking client orders
- Following orders through production to ensure on time delivery
- Following up with clients after order is delivered to ensure customer satisfaction
- Obtaining additional business from current clients
- Obtaining and following up referral business from clients
- Participating on the marketing team to create new marketing programs

Goals

Following are the sales goals set out for Associate.
Performance reviews, salary adjustments and other
elements of employment and promotion will be based in
part on accomplishing the following:

- To increase referral business by 15% over the next
  calendar year

- To increase new outside customers by 7 per
  month

- To increase sales by 12% over calendar 1997

- To increase close ratio from 23% to 30%

Ownership of Materials

Acme is sole owner of all marketing materials, ideas,
mailing lists, customer lists, and all other materials used to
promote Acme. Associate acknowledges the
confidentiality of all such materials and agrees to keep all
materials safe and to prevent them from falling in the
hands of anyone not connected with Acme with a right to
know. Associate agrees that upon termination of his
employment with Acme, all such materials shall
immediately be returned to Acme.

Compensation

Associate shall be compensated as follows:

- Salary of $2000 per month

- Commission of 10% of all sales in excess of $6000
  per month

- Bonus of an additional 5% of all sales in excess of
  $10,000 per month

- Annual bonus of $5000 if annual sales exceed
  $125,000

- For purposes of all above calculations, only sales made directly by Associate are counted

Termination
This agreement is an employment at will. It may be terminated by either party at any time without cause or notice. In the event of termination, Associate shall receive all commissions due him based on sales made (signed orders with deposit checks in hand) at the point of termination. Upon termination, all materials shall be returned to Acme.

Entire Agreement
This agreement represents all elements of an agreement between the parties.

Agreed:

Associate   Acme Bowling Balls

_____   _____

Leon Frank   *Jim Acme – President*

Date _____

Sample Service Agreement

_____ (CLIENT) retains Acme Computer Service (ACME) according to the following terms:

Scope of Work
ACME will maintain and service all equipment listed below as follows:

- Twice annually, starting at the signing of this agreement, ACME will perform preventive maintenance according to factory schedules for each piece of equipment

- On-call services and repairs as needed. ACME will respond within 24 hours of telephone notification during normal business hours to any service problem. ACME will provide CLIENT with priority service ahead of all other non-Service Agreement clients at all times. CLIENT will contact ACME at 410-123-4567.

List of Equipment
Following is a list of equipment covered by this agreement. CLIENT may add additional equipment at any time. When CLIENT gives ACME written description of new equipment to be added to this Agreement, ACME will notify CLIENT within 5 days the amount of the additional charge for adding such equipment to this Service Agreement.

1. Equipment Description A

2. Equipment Description B

3. Equipment Description C

4. Equipment Description D

Provision for Unavailable Parts and Supplies

Acme will in all cases attempt to return equipment to working order as quickly as possible. However, in cases where needed parts or supplies are unavailable, there may be a delay in returning equipment to operational until such parts or supplies are obtained. *(Note: cover yourself for any contingencies here)*

Fees and Payment

Acme will be paid a retainer of $xxxx per month for the services covered in this Agreement. This fee covers all labor, travel to and from CLIENT's location(s) and ACME's shop supplies necessary to complete service. Parts needed for repairs will be billed at cost at the end of each month in addition to the retainer amount.

Termination

This Agreement will remain in force for one year from the date of signing. It may not be terminated before that date unless agreed to by both parties in writing. At the end of one year, it will be automatically extended for one more year unless terminated by either party in writing prior to 30 days from the end date.

Note: make clear restrictions against early termination, especially if you are giving up front labor based on the entire year contract being fulfilled. In this sample, Acme is providing full service of all the client's equipment at the start of the agreement. Acme cannot afford to provide the full equipment service and then have the client cancel after paying only one month's retainer. On the other end, I like agreements that are self-perpetuating so the client does not have to make a decision whether to continue retaining you. The way this is written, the client has to make a decision to terminate and notify you.

Trade Show Contact Information

When exhibiting at Trade Shows, identify visitors to your booth who are viable prospects for your company. When you identify them, use this opportunity while you have them at hand to get the critical information that you will need to sell to them after the show. Create a form to fill out for each prospect. Get all of the following information as well as any other specific items you need to know for your company.

1. Contact Name

2. Company

3. Mailing address to reach contact

4. Telephone number to reach contact

5. Type of company

6. Which of your products and services are appropriate for them

7. Who is the appropriate decision maker to purchase your products and services – how do you reach them

8. Whose products and services are they using now

9. Are they happy with their current vendor

10. What current needs can your products and services fill

11. What basic information you need about their company – size, location, branches, products, etc.

12. What do you need to do to sell them on switching to your products and services

After the show, use this information to develop a marketing strategy to reach each prospect. Now armed with this information, you should be able to go directly to the correct person in their company and demonstrate how your products or services can meet their specific needs – translation: a sale for your company.

Sample Customer Interview Script

Hello, this is Leon Frank, from Acme Software Company. We are calling all of our customers and talking to them about how we can serve them better. Do you have a few minutes to talk to me?

What do you like best about doing business with Acme Software?

What do you like least?

How can we improve our service to you?

Do you shop with [name of competitor]?

If so, what do they offer that we don't?

What additional services (or products) could we provide?

George Kaslowsky, our company president specifically told me to ask you if there was anything you would like to tell him directly.

Would you please tell me a little about your company?
Who makes the purchase decisions?
What size is your company?
What products do you sell?
What trade magazines do you subscribe to?
What trade shows do you go to?